GLORIOUS COLOR

KAFFE FASSETT
PHOTOGRAPHY BY STEVE LOVI

GLORIOUS COLOR

Sources of Inspiration for Knitting
and Needlepoint, with 17 Projects

BY KAFFE FASSETT
PHOTOGRAPHY BY STEVE LOVI

CLARKSON N. POTTER, INC./PUBLISHERS
DISTRIBUTED BY CROWN PUBLISHERS, INC., NEW YORK

Published by Clarkson N. Potter, Inc.,
225 Park Avenue South, New York, New York 10003

CLARKSON N. POTTER, POTTER, and colophon
are trademarks of Clarkson N. Potter, Inc.

Manufactured in Spain

Library of Congress Cataloging-in-Publication Data
Fassett, Kaffe.
Glorious color : sources for knitting and needlepoint from the
Victoria and Albert Museum / by Kaffe Fassett : photography
by Steve Lovi.
p.   cm.
ISBN 0-517-56988-4 : $27.50
1. Knitting—Patterns. 2. Canvas embroidery—Patterns.
3. Decoration and ornament. I. Victoria and Albert Museum.
II. Title.
TT820.F335 1988
746.43'2—dc19   88-12685

10 9 8 7 6 5 4 3 2 1

First Edition

*Title page: Detail of a nineteenth-century Coalport
melon plate from the V&A collection.*

*Opposite title page: Detail of Kaffe Fassett's
Melon tapestry (pages 126 and 127).*

CONTENTS

INTRODUCTION

Barefoot California boy hits London – stays twenty-three years. When simply stated, the idea of exchanging the beaches, glamorous life and affluence of California for damp, grey London does raise a few questions. Looking back at my childhood, I find the seeds of my British adventure in the nostalgic images of Old England gleaned from stories like *Winnie the Pooh* and *Mary Poppins*, the tales of Oscar Wilde and Dickens, and the operettas of Gilbert and Sullivan. They had furnished me with a cosy world of expectations to be verified.

This early enthusiasm for British culture was later enhanced by mingling with the many British travellers in my parents' restaurant and enjoying their witty repartee. Later, reading the works of Christopher Isherwood, whom I had met at a dinner party in San Francisco, and discovering the paintings of Turner, Constable and Augustus John made a trip to England inevitable.

FROM CALIFORNIA TO BRITAIN

In 1964 I flew over to experience the reality of this great dream that had grown in my head. The brilliant engineer Jeremy Fry was one of the English people I had met in California, and he and his wife Camilla offered me my first home in Britain.

Arriving in London before going on to the Frys' in Bath, I was initially shocked by how clean and light-coloured the buildings were. I had expected dingy, sooty, Dickensian exteriors; and, although I would later discover plenty of these, it was the creamy stucco and, above all, the bright pastel-painted houses that caught my eye. The weather helped too; it was a glowing autumn – my favourite time of year – and London was bathed in a warm pinky-gold light. The smells and sights and voices of that London autumn gave substance to my inner picture and confirmed my youthful Anglophilia. Piccadilly Circus, draped with Beatle look-alikes, exuberant Carnaby Street and the King's Road, eating steak and kidney pies bought from street vendors and walking through lush parks and gardens – all filled my first days. I delighted in the flowers tumbling from bank window boxes and was constantly discovering odd little squares, crescents and beautiful Wren churches.

On excursions out of London I marvelled at the exquisite colouring in grand English gardens, my favourite being Hidcote, in the Cotswolds. Best of all there was listening to the song of British English, in all its rich variety.

Later, when I moved down to Bath, the Frys introduced me to a delightfully diverse group of people with their own worlds for me to explore. Bath itself was existing in another century to my eyes. The imposing, stylish Bath stone crescents and terraces thrilled me. I spent days drawing elegant Georgian terraces. Then the American Museum, near Bath, commissioned a series of my drawings for their guidebook.

MOVING TO LONDON

After six months in Bath, I moved back to London to set up a studio and do some serious painting, as I began to realize I was going to be around for some time. Lansdowne Crescent, in Notting Hill Gate, was a fateful choice, being on the doorstep of the Portobello Road market.

I had never before heard of this famous flea market, which now burst upon my senses like a toy-filled attic to a child – miles of stalls laden with china ware, carpets, furnishings and fabrics of every description. Cockney stall holders there taught me to bargain. Even with my

This page: In California at eighteen, incurably romantic with cow's pelvic bone and Ethiopian necklace (far left). At twenty-seven visiting Widcombe Manor, Bath (left). In my Notting Hill studio, working on a triptych of Portobello objects, wearing the bold stripes of my first knitting design (below far left). Bill Gibb and me with one of my early shell paintings, 1968 (below left).

meagre artist's income, there was treasure to be had, and the amount you could get for £5 could hardly be hauled home. Embroidered tablecloths, wonderful decorated china, shirts and ties, old maps, books, postcards and lace all became the raw material for many of my still life paintings and drawings.

DISCOVERING THE V&A

In search of visual stimuli, I went on to visit other markets like Bermondsey and Church Street, in Marylebone. Then, one amazing day, I was taken by a friend to the Victoria and Albert Museum. It struck me instantly as a condensed version of all the delights of the London experience, with the added bonus of fine historical treasures and collections from the Orient and the Near East. This great

celebration of the world's decorative art is what finally made me realize that my heart lay in this area. I was painting so-called fine art, but longing to explore the joyous domains of decorated objects.

Here under one roof were carpets, embroideries, jewelled boxes, Indian miniatures, costumes and fans of many ages, highly decorated musical instruments and, most exciting of all to my eye, room after room of beautifully patterned china. I returned again and again in those early years and dragged visiting travellers there as a highlight of their London tour.

THE ADVENTURE OF KNITTING

Soon after setting up in Lansdowne Crescent, I met the noted Scottish designer Bill Gibb, who was just finishing his

and commissioned me to do a patterned waistcoat for her next issue.

While I was working on this commission, I visited Bill Gibb's family on a farm in Scotland. I felt that he himself would make a wonderful story – child raised in the isolated Scottish countryside dreams of costumes and clothes and comes to London to discover he has a talent for creating a very original look. I introduced him to Judy and prompted her to do something for him. She said to me, 'If you do the knitting to go with his outfits I'll sell the story to the *Sunday Times* or *Vogue*'.

Excited to have a chance to do such a creative project, I rushed to Billy and said we must do something really over the top. This was an opportunity to throw off the restraints of the day. Designers then were very much influenced by the smooth, impersonal look of the early Sixties – prim little coats, pillbox hats, patent leather, and the like. As steeped as I was in the exuberance of the Portobello Road market and the rich decoration in every corner of the V&A, I envisaged a glorious mixture of patterns, reacting against the streamlined current fashions.

I dragged Billy off to examine the intricate details of the Indian primitive paintings and the rich colours and patterns of china in the V&A. Judy would often join us in these endless walks through the imagination-expanding collections. The cases of the museum became like so many flowerbeds in a favourite garden that you never tire of exploring.

Billy threw himself into the new project, designing great pleated skirts in ancient tartans with inset panels of flower prints, topped off with billowy-sleeved blouses in yet another rich pattern. I then made knitted jackets, waistcoats and panels for coats which echoed all the patterns and colours of his fabric combinations.

When the drawings were completed and tagged with fabric and knitted swatches, we delivered the collection to *Vogue* for first refusal. They offered us

training and opening his first fashion shop. He took me to Scotland on a tweed-buying trip, and it was there I found the beautiful, subtly coloured yarns that started me knitting. When I had completed my first striped cardigan, using twenty colours, I took it to show Judy Brittain (then the editor of *Vogue Knitting* in London). She recognized something in that primitive first attempt that she felt could affect knitting for years to come

This page: These three excellent flower sources give you a taste of the infinite variety of this subject in the V&A. The painted fabric (below far left) and the detailed urn (below left) create a delicate pastel mood, while the china plaque (left) has the kind of drama I have put into the Flower Trellis carpet (page 114).

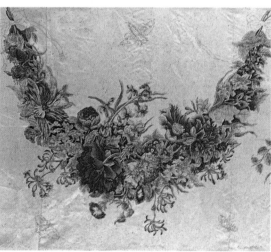

four colour pages! When made up, the collection got a lot of attention, and our first ensemble – a skirt, blouse and knitted waistcoat – was chosen as 'Outfit of the Year' for the Museum of Costume in Bath.

DELIGHTFUL SOURCES

After these encouraging beginnings, I continued with my knitting, working on a series of one-off garments. I also started doing needlepoint and found it a fascinating, though quite different, vehicle for colour and pattern.

My search for design inspiration for my textiles took me to the V&A again and again. Photographer Steve Lovi was another friend who enthusiastically accompanied me on my rambles through the V&A. He had moved to London from California soon after I settled in Notting Hill, and his perceptive eye guided many of my projects from potential disaster to

Right: Shell urn from the V&A (see V&A sources list, page 156 for details).

Far right: My watercolour of a shell urn. Shells have always been one of my favourite decorative themes.

Below right: A watercolour from my sketchbook of a large cloisonné vase from the British Museum.

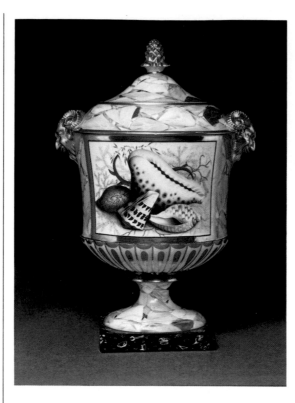

satisfactory conclusion. He always encouraged me to go further, use more colour and strive for richer, more unusual effects.

During my first years in London, I would also spend hours alone in the V&A sketching bits of mosaic, china pots, textiles – anything with a pattern became grist to my mill. I ate, slept and drank patterns, and the V&A was one large storehouse of them.

Many classic themes fed me with ideas. For instance, shells beautifully depicted first influenced my still lifes, then later my knitting and needlepoint. Something else that caught my eye in those early days, because of its graceful shape and design potential, was the painted fan. The V&A boasts some striking examples, from Oriental to European styles, some with carefully rendered details and others with bold patterns, like the Japanese cloud fan shown here which really inspires me.

There is an invaluable lesson to be learned from great diverse collections like that of the V&A. To be confronted with so many examples of decoration, from the most boldly exuberant to the most subtly intricate, including china, mosaics, textiles and carved ivory, de-

monstrates that any pattern idea can be used in any way you fancy. Whether doing needlepoint, knitting or any other creative work, we should avail ourselves of the wealth of pattern that can be found in a first-class decorative arts museum.

This book is published to coincide with a V&A exhibition containing a selection of my work dating back to my arrival in Britain. To prepare for the book, I had the great luxury of spending a year working quite specifically from

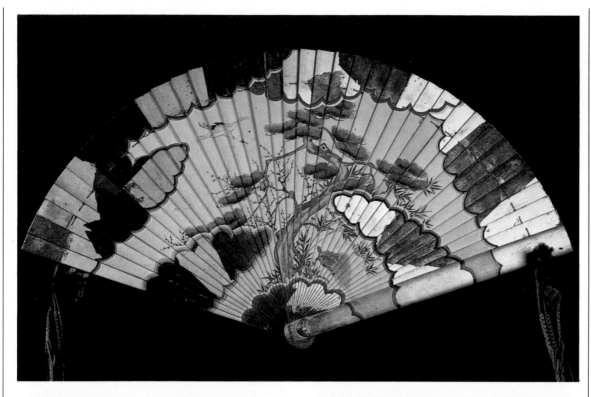

some inspired sources at the V&A to point out what a treasure house it is (see page 156 for a list of the V&A objects included).

Also included in the show and in this book are many other of my textile ideas which are loosely based on a wide range of sources – proof that any would-be designer has an infinite range of ideas to work from. Many of the projects for which instructions are given in detail are pastiches – fairly literal interpretations of the original sources. They illustrate a way to work directly from sources; more often however, in my work, only

vague references to the sources can be discerned.

As a designer becomes more confident in his or her work, the connection with the original source gets much more obscure, and the work becomes more personal. By contrast, working closely from a beautiful object that has caught your eye can serve the same function as working on a professionally designed kit. It gives you the experience, perhaps for the first time, of working with a good number of colours and a balanced design. From there it is a short step to creating your own personal statements.

STRIPES AND STEPS

The stripe started my knitting adventure when I purchased twenty colours of Shetland yarn from a Scottish mill and put them all into my first cardigan. I remember dreaming of striated sandstone and ancient biblical robes, while conjuring up those multi-changing stripes.

Stripes are so direct and cutting that they can widen or magically slenderize an object; they move around objects describing their shapes. They can undulate or swirl, becoming such an intricately marbled pattern that we hardly perceive them as stripes.

As I travel the world observing patterns in other cultures, I notice many variations on this basic pattern. The bold circus and shop front awnings catch the eye with their simple, direct contrasts.

Left: The Jewel Stripe shawl with some of the pots that inspired it. Intense jewel colours make this fan (below) a delightful source for the textile artist.

*Previous page: The
Jewel Stripe shawl
comes alive in the
company of the
glowing colours in
Kay Gallwey's
studio.*

Beach chairs and hammocks often feature brilliant stripes; clothes, furnishings and natural objects like feathers, stones and shells all constantly surprise us with never-ending uses of stripes.

JEWEL STRIPE SHAWL

Great sheets of fabric are wonderful to knit. You just set out with a mass of gorgeous colours, a pattern structure to hang them on – and let loose, working back and forth across your rows, spinning your magic web.

The Jewel Stripe shawl, with its blocks of stripes, is great fun to knit. You estab-

lish the first rows of your blocks of stripes across the row and then knit away until it is time to make decisions about the next lot of colours. I varied the scale of the blocks to keep the design rich and unexpected and worked in the occasional change of tone within each block.

My colours were directly inspired by the intense, glowing glazes of nineteenth- and twentieth-century pottery at the V&A. If you want to attempt these colours, be sure to keep them dark and rich. The important thing is not to dilute the mysterious depth of tone by a shocking light colour – one of the commonest mistakes made in design.

YARNS FOR JEWEL STRIPE SHAWL
Average yarn weight used – chunky (bulky)
Approx 850g (30oz) in a mixture of yarns and colours in dark shades A
Approx 850g (30oz) in a mixture of yarns and colours in medium shades B

NEEDLES
One 5mm (US size 8) and one 6mm (US size 10) circular needle 100cm (39″) long
or size to obtain correct tension (gauge)

MEASUREMENTS
103cm (41″) wide 224cm (89½″) long

TENSION (GAUGE)
16 sts and 18 rows to 10cm (4″) over colour patt on 6mm (US size 10) needles
Check your tension (gauge) before beginning.

NOTES
Use a separate length of each colour for each square. When working vertical stripes in a single square, carry colour not in use across back of work, weaving it around working yarn.

DIMENSIONS OF SQUARES
The striped square patt is made by working bands of squares across the width of the shawl. The number of sts and rows in each of the 3 square sizes is as foll:
SMALL SQUARES
Each small square is worked over 10 sts and 10 rows. Each vertical stripe is 2 sts

wide and each horizontal stripe is 2 rows deep.

MEDIUM-SIZED SQUARES
Each medium-sized square is worked over 20 sts and 20 rows. Each vertical stripe is 4 sts wide and each horizontal stripe is 4 rows deep.

LARGE SQUARES
Each large square is worked over 40 sts and 36 rows. Each vertical stripe is 8 sts wide and each horizontal stripe is 6 rows deep.

TO MAKE
Using 5mm (US size 8) circular needle and A, cast on 160 sts. Working back and forth in rows throughout and using a different shade of A, work 3 rows in garter st (knit every row). Using B, purl 2 rows and knit 1 row.

FIRST BAND OF SQUARES
Change to 6mm (US size 10) circular needle and beg working colour patt in st st as foll:

1st row (RS) Using a different shade of A and B for each square and working each square over 20 sts, K4A, (4B, 4A) twice, *20B, 4A, (4B, 4A) twice, rep from * twice more, 20A. Positions of 8 medium-sized squares set across row.

2nd row Keeping to same or similar shades of A and B for each square until first band of squares is complete, P20A, *4A, (4B, 4A) twice, 20B, rep from * twice more, 4A, (4B, 4A) twice.

3rd and 4th rows As first and 2nd rows.

5th row K4A, (4B, 4A) twice, *20A, 4A, (4B, 4A) twice, rep from * twice more, 20B.

6th row P20B, *4A, (4B, 4A) twice, 20A, rep from * twice more, 4A, (4B, 4A) twice.

7th and 8th rows As 5th and 6th rows.

9th-16th rows As first-8th rows.

17th-20th rows As first-4th rows.
This completes first band of squares.

2ND BAND OF SQUARES
21st row Using a different shade of A and B for each square and working each square over 10 sts, K2B, (2A, 2B) twice, *10A, 2A, (2B, 2A) twice*, rep from * to * once more, 10B, 2A, (2B, 2A) twice, rep from * to * 4 times more, 10A. Positions of 16 small squares set across row.

22nd row Keeping to same or similar shades of A and B for each square until 2nd band of squares is complete, *P10A, 2A, (2B, 2A) twice*, rep from * to * 4 times more, 10B, **2A, (2B, 2A) twice, 10A**, rep from ** to ** once more, 2B, (2A, 2B) twice.

23rd row K2B, (2A, 2B) twice, *10B, 2A, (2B, 2A) twice*, rep from * to * once more, 10A, 2A, (2B, 2A) twice, rep from * to * 4 times more, 10B.

24th row Working each st in same shade as last row, purl.

25th-28th rows As 21st-24th rows.

29th and 30th rows As 21st and 22nd.
This completes 2nd band of squares.

3RD-6TH BANDS OF SQUARES
Work 2 more bands of small squares each over 10 rows, foll diagram for shades and direction of stripes.
Work 2 bands of medium-sized squares, each over 20 rows, foll diagram for shades and direction of stripes.

7TH BAND OF SQUARES
91st row Using a different shade of A and B for each square and working each square over 40 sts, *K40A, 8B, (8A, 8B) twice, rep from * once more. Positions of 4 large squares set across row.

92nd row Keeping to same or similar shades of A and B for each square until 7th band of squares is complete and working each st in same colour as last row, purl.

Left: Detail of the Jewel Stripe shawl, with its great slabs of deep, pure colour. Another striking colouring for the shawl would be chalky light shell tones, or even black, white and greys.

93rd-96th rows Rep 91st and 92nd rows
twice more.

97th row *K40B, 8B, (8A, 8B) twice, rep
from * once more.

98th row Working each st in same shade
as last row, purl.

99th-102nd rows Rep 97th and 98th rows
twice more.

103rd-126th rows Rep 91st-102nd rows
twice more.

Cont in this way, foll diagram for sizes of
squares, shades and direction of stripes,
until all the bands of squares have been
worked, so ending with a WS row.

Change to 5mm (US size 8) circular
needle and using B, work 2 rows in garter
st, then purl 1 row.

Using A, purl 3 rows.

Using a different shade of A, cast (bind)
off loosely.

FINISHING

Work edging along 2 long sides of shawl
by picking up sts as foll:

Using 5mm (US size 8) circular needle

JOYOUS STRIPES

What is it about Venetian and Dutch striped glass that strikes such a chord of delight! Perhaps it is like the pretty candies and glass marbles whose luminous depths intrigued us as children. Whatever it is, I am always inspired by this theme. In fact, revisiting the collection at the V&A makes me want to start all over again dreaming up more frothy confections of stripes.

The variations here are so intriguing – how merrily these simple lines can dance together! I particularly like the mixture of Venetian glass with the Chinese pot using that mad spiralling stripe. The main thing to remember when designing your own stripes is to get enough variations going to express the delicious complexity these simple stripes can achieve.

ISLAMIC STRIPE PATCH CREWNECK

I love the wealth of stripes to be found in the Islamic world. Every time I have strolled through a bazaar or souk, I have been thrilled at the endless variety of striped fabrics, carpets and objects. Pure, exquisitely simple striped bowls (pages 20 and 21) were the main inspiration for this crewneck. The patched robes of the Sufis gave me a structure, and the rich colouring of Islamic pottery on a stone and sand base the colour scheme.

The patches of this crewneck are charted in detail, whereas the striped background is left for you to fill in as you see fit. The main rule is not to work too many rows with any one colour, so as to keep the variations rolling. No two knitters will combine yarns in the same sequence, making each sweater unique.

YARNS FOR ISLAMIC STRIPE PATCH CREWNECK

Average yarn weight used – double knitting (knitting worsted)
Rowan *Fleck DK* in the foll 4 colours:
  A (#82F) beige – 150g (5½oz)
  B (#64F) grey – 100g (3½oz)
  C (#56F) royal blue – 50g (1¾oz)
  D (#62F) black – 50g (1¾oz)

Left: This deliciously varied grouping of stripes shows you the exciting possibilities of this simple theme. It was fun to place these classic glass stripes on striped textiles.

and B and with RS facing, pick up and K360 sts evenly along edge (approx 11 sts for every 12 row ends). Work 2 rows in garter st. Cast (bind) off loosely.

Rowan *Light Tweed* in the foll 7 colours:
  E (#222) lakeland – 100g (3½oz)
  F (#205) autumn – 100g (3½oz)
  G (#202) champagne – 50g (1¾oz)
  H (#201) scoured – 75g (2¾oz)
  I (#203) pebble – 75g (2¾oz)
  J (#220) jade – 25g (1oz)
  L (#221) Pacific – 25g (1oz)
Rowan *Designer DK* in the foll 6 colours:
  M (#616) taupe – 100g (3½oz)
  N (#118) dusty mauve – 50g (1¾oz)
  O (#628) navy – 100g (3½oz)
  Q (#65) slate – 50g (1¾oz)
  R (#625) charcoal – 50g (1¾oz)
  S (#501) hyacinth – 50g (1¾oz)
Rowan *Lightweight DK* in the foll 3 colours:
  T (#98) peat – 25g (1oz)
  U (#47) pale blue – 25g (1oz)
  V (#416) ocean – 25g (1oz)

NEEDLES
One pair each of 3¾mm (US size 5) and 4½mm (US size 7) needles *or size to obtain correct tension (gauge)*
One 3¾mm (US size 5) circular needle 40cm (15½″) long

SIZES AND MEASUREMENTS
To fit 86-91[96-102:107-112]cm (34-36 [38-40:42-44]″) bust or chest
Actual width across back 55[60:65]cm (22[24:26]″)
Length to shoulder 61[63:64]cm (24¼[25:25½]″)
Sleeve length 44cm (17½″)
Figures for larger sizes are given in square brackets; where there is only one set of figures, it applies to all sizes.

TENSION (GAUGE)
21 sts and 25 rows to 10cm (4″) over colour patt on 4½mm (US size 7) needles
Check your tension (gauge) before beginning.

NOTES
Use a separate length of each colour for each area of background stripes, twisting yarns when changing colours to avoid holes. When working vertical stripes of patches, carry patch colour not in use loosely across back of patch weaving it around working yarn.

Read chart from right to left for RS (knit) rows and from left to right for WS (purl) rows.
Use 1 strand of yarn where there is only one letter to represent the colour and 2 strands of yarn where there are two letters, i.e. 'GF' means 1 strand each of G and F.

BACK AND FRONT
Back and front are worked in one piece beg at lower back.
BACK
Using 3¾mm (US size 5) needles and A, cast on 103[109:115] sts.
Work 19 rows in K1, P1 rib patt in stripes as foll:
2 rows A, 3 rows EF, 2 rows M, 2 rows EG, 1 row N, 1 row GH, 3 rows A, 2 rows B, 2 rows N, 1 row M.
Next row (inc row) Using M, rib 9[6:7], make 1 st by picking up horizontal loop lying before next st and working into the back of it – called make 1 –, (rib 7[6:5], make 1) 12[16:20] times, rib 10[7:8]. 116[126:136] sts.
*Change to 4½mm (US size 7) needles and beg with a K row, work 14[18:22] rows in st st in stripes as foll:
0[0:1] row EG, 0[0:3] rows EF, 0[1:1] row M, 0[1:1] row N, 0[1:1] row EG, 0[1:1] row EF, 1 row M, 2 rows EF, 1 row A, 2 rows EH, 1 row B, 1 row A, 2 rows FG, 3 rows EF, 1 row EH, so ending with a WS row.
Beg with a K row, cont in st st, working background in random stripes (using colours A, B, M and N single and colours E, F, G, H and I double for random stripes) and foll chart from 23rd chart row for patches and foll patch colour chart for patch stripe colours*, until 138th chart row has been completed.
NECK SHAPING
Divide for neck on next row as foll:
139th chart row (RS) Patt 48[52:55] sts, cast (bind) off 20[22:26] centre sts, patt to end.
140th chart row Patt to neck edge, slip rem sts (right shoulder) onto a spare needle (see foll Note). 48[52:55] sts at each side of neck.
Note *If desired, work both sides of neck at same time with separate balls of yarn.*

LEFT BACK NECK EDGE
Keeping patt correct, cast (bind) off 6 sts at beg of next row (neck edge) and 3 sts at beg of foll alternate row. 39[43:46] sts. Work 1 row without shaping. Mark each end of last row for shoulder line.

LEFT FRONT NECK EDGE
Cont on these sts for front, working from shoulder to lower edge, matching background stripes by working same stripes as for back in reverse order and foll chart from 145th chart row for patches and patch colour chart in reverse order for patch stripe colours, AND AT THE SAME TIME shape neck edge as foll:
Work 5 rows without shaping.
Inc 1 st at end of next row (neck edge), then inc 1 st at neck edge on every alternate row 5[5:6] times more. Work 1 row without shaping. Cast on 2 sts at end of next row, then cast on at neck edge on every alternate row 2 sts once and 3 sts once, so ending with a WS row. 52 [56:60] sts. Slip sts onto a spare needle.

RIGHT BACK NECK EDGE
With WS facing, rejoin yarn to neck edge of sts at other side of neck and cast (bind) off 6 sts, patt to end.
Keeping patt correct, work 1 row without shaping. Cast (bind) off 3 sts at beg of next row. 39[43:46] sts.
Work 2 rows without shaping. Mark each end of last row for shoulder line.

RIGHT FRONT NECK EDGE
Cont on these sts for front, reversing colour patt as for other side of neck, AND AT THE SAME TIME shape neck as foll:
Work 4 rows without shaping. Work as for left front neck from ** to **, so ending with a RS row. 52[56:60] sts.
Work 1 row without shaping.

FRONT
Join both sides of neck on next row as foll:
167th[167th:169th] chart row Patt across

Left: The Islamic Stripe Patch crewneck with the Squares and Stripe Patch shawls which were worked in my usual triangular shawl shape (see Persian Poppy shawl, page 79).

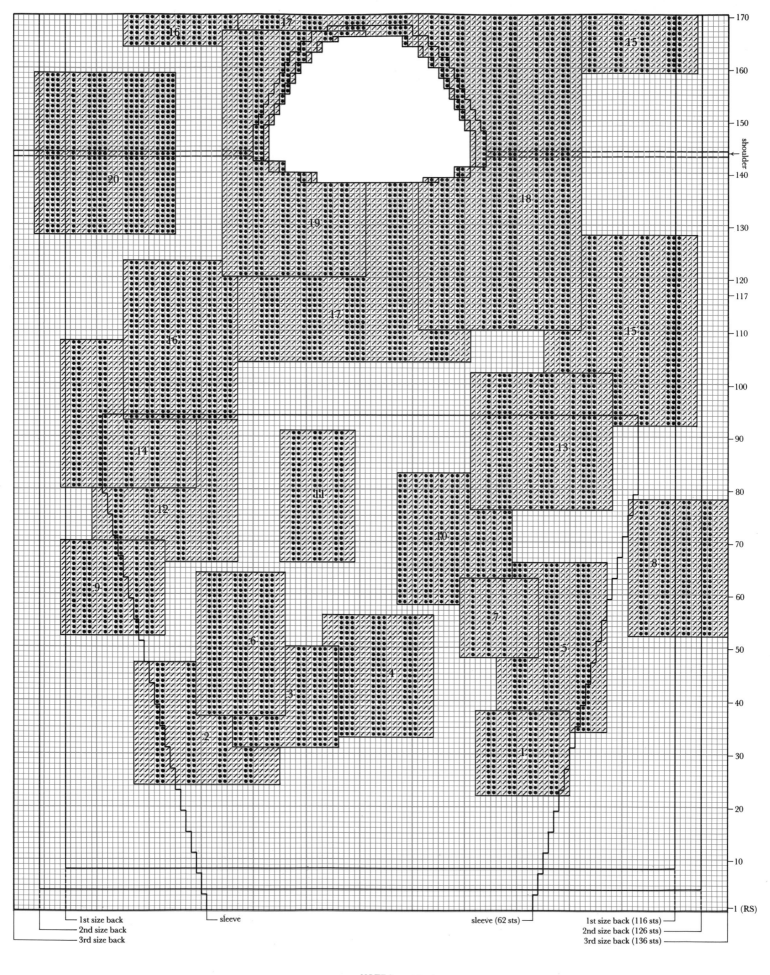

170
160
shoulder
150
140
130
120
117
110
100
90
80
70
60
50
40
30
20
10
1 (RS)

1st size back
2nd size back
3rd size back
sleeve
sleeve (62 sts)
1st size back (116 sts)
2nd size back (126 sts)
3rd size back (136 sts)

NOTE See patch colour
chart for actual patch
colours and see
instructions for background
colours.

☐ = background colours
▨ = light patch stripes
▣ = dark patch stripes

PATCH COLOURS

	rows	◻	●
Patch 1	23-38	M	C
Patch 2	25-47	EE	D
Patch 3	32-50	N	O
Patch 4	34-56	B	Q
Patch 5	35-38	GH	R
	39-51	GH	O
	52-58	GG	O
	59-62	GF	O
	63-66	FF	O
Patch 6	38-43	HH	C
	44-52	GH	C
	53-56	GG	C
	57-58	A	C
	59-64	M	C
Patch 7	49-51	V	O
	52-56	EV	O
	57-58	JV	O
	59-63	JL	O
Patch 8	53-66	B	FT
	67-69	B	RT
	70-78	B	R
Patch 9	53-56	GL	Q
	57-58	EL	Q
	59-63	EL	O
	64-70	FL	O
Patch 10	59-66	EH	S
	67-73	B	S
	74-80	B	C
	81-83	B	O
Patch 11	67-79	GU	R
	80-82	GG	R
	83-85	GH	R
	86-91	HH	R
Patch 12	67-93	N	O
Patch 13	77-102	A	Q
Patch 14	81-82	VV	S
	83-85	HV	C
	86-89	JV	C
	90-91	LV	C
	92	LL	C
	93-95	IL	C
	96-100	FL	C
	101-108	EL	C
Patch 15	93-106	EU	O
	107	UV	O
	108-109	IV	O
	110-122	GH	O
	123-128	HH	O
Patch 16	94-109	B	FT
	110	BG	FT
	111	BG	R
	112-114	GU	R
	115-118	HU	R
	119-123	HH	R
Patch 17	105-121	M	O
	122-125	N	O
	126-138	M	O
Patch 18	111-114	B	R
Patch 19	121-124	JJ	S
	125-129	JL	C
	130-131	LL	C
	132-144	HL	C

Rep patch colours in reverse order for front.

NOTE Where there are 2 letters, 2 strands of yarn are used, i.e. 'EE' means 2 strands of E.

sts at right side of neck, cast on 12[14:16] sts for centre front neck, patt across sts on spare needle. 116[126:136] sts.

Cont in colour patt foll chart until 170th chart row has been completed, so ending with a WS row.

Cont foll chart from 117th chart row backwards matching background stripes and patch stripes as before, until 23rd chart row has been completed. Work 14[18:22] rows more in background stripes as for back, so ending with a RS row.

Change to 3¾mm (US size 5) needles and dec for rib as foll:

<u>Next row</u> (dec row) Using M, P9[6:7], P2 tog, (P6[5:4], P2 tog) 12[16:20] times, P[9:6:7]. 103[109:115] sts.

Below: Detail of Islamic Stripe Patch crewneck; and Stripe Patch shawl, Squares shawl and Islamic Stripe Patch crewneck.

Work 19 rows in rib patt as for back, reversing order of stripes.

Using A, cast (bind) off loosely in rib.

SLEEVES

<u>Note</u> *If desired, work both sleeves at same time with separate balls of yarn.*

Using 3¾mm (US size 5) needles and A, cast on 47 sts.

Work 19 rows in rib patt as for back, so ending with a RS row.

<u>Next row</u> (inc row) Using M, (rib 3, make 1) 15 times, rib 2. 62 sts.

Work in colour patt as for back from * to * foll instructions for *3rd size*, AND AT THE SAME TIME shape sleeve by inc 1 st at each end of every 4th row until there are 102 sts. Work without shaping until 94th chart row has been completed or until sleeve is required length. Cast (bind) off.

NECKBAND

Press all pieces lightly on WS with a warm iron over a damp cloth, omitting ribbing.

Using 3¾mm (US size 5) circular needle and A and with RS facing, beg at left shoulder line and pick up and K62[64:70] sts evenly along front neck and 40[42:46] sts across back neck. 102[106:116] sts.

Work 6 rounds in K1, P1 rib.

Using Q, work 3 rounds more in rib.

Using Q, cast (bind) off loosely in rib.

FINISHING

Mark back and front at side edges 24cm (9½″) from shoulder line. Using back-stitch, join cast (bound) off edge of sleeves between markers, matching centre of top of sleeve to shoulder line. Join side and sleeve seams, using back-stitch for st st and invisible seam for rib. Press seams lightly on WS with a warm iron over a damp cloth, omitting ribbing.

THREE ROW STRIPE

Probably the most fascinating thing about a simple pattern is its endless potential for variation. Bands of solid colour are the simplest of the simple when it comes to colour layouts in tex-

Left: Variations of the simple Three Row Stripe, the Toothed Stripe waistcoat (one of my most popular designs from 'Glorious Knitting'), a tweedy variation of the Romeo and Juliet coat (page 35), fresh stripes in a Maltese doorway and swirling glass stripes against textile designer Richard Womersley's woven stripes.

Page 28: Detail of the Carpet coat from 'Glorious Knitting' in a rich tobacco and gunmetal grey colourway.

Page 29: The kilim-inspired shape of my Carpet design is a perfect vehicle for striped colourings.

tiles. My Three Row Stripe is just what it says – three rows each of colour after colour, until contrasting and merging colours are built up to a rich arrangement. It was actually inspired by the vivid stripes of Korean national costumes, with their boldly contrasting reds, creams, greens and blues.

Paradoxically, my most successful versions of this pattern use very closely related shades like misty greys, muddy pastels, looking a bit like slabs of stone, or soft, muted shades of green, all toned to suggest a hillside of trees in late spring.

TOOTHED STRIPE

In complete contrast to the straightforward Three Row Stripe is the Toothed Stripe. This jagged, lively vehicle for colour lends itself to many interpretations. I spotted the idea first on an embroidery from the Mediterranean. It was done in sharp, spicy colours, so my original version contrasted pastels with deeper, brighter colours. Later I played with closer harmonies like jades, blues, greens and dark mossy tones with tweedy browns. Flame reds and turquoises were used for a bold V-neck.

Although this stripe appears complex, it has been attempted with gleeful results by knitters all over the world, including beginners. I have had the immense pleasure of seeing hundreds of unique, personal colourways in this pattern, often done by people who had not knitted in years or were quite frightened of using colour before reading my earlier book, *Glorious Knitting*. One stunning example of this pattern was knitted in a blaze of colour as a first sweater by a Portland, Oregon, knitter.

CARPET STRIPE

Of all the possible variations on stripes, the Carpet Stripe is the one I keep returning to for my jackets and coats. Inspired by a woven kilim carpet, the big pineapple shapes become a vigorous way to break up stripes of colours. The pattern (charted in *Glorious Knitting*) can be quickly memorized and has the kind of

Left: The easy-to-knit vertical Zigzag in several colourings and an example of the horizontal landscape quality of the Jack's Back Stripe, both in 'Glorious Knitting'.

Right: Different scales and colourings of the Steps pattern, with a Maltese castellated roofline showing an early architectural interpretation of this theme.

rhythm that keeps you rolling along. The big coats, in particular, go much faster than at first one would suspect, with only three or four changes of colour at one time across the row and sometimes many rows per area of the same colour. The actual knitting progresses at a rapid pace on the large needles using chunky yarns. I have completed one in a week.

Starting with about three groups of colours in various tones and textures helps with the organizing of the Carpet Stripe pattern. Knit these groups into each section of the design, dropping in the occasional line or two of a different 'kick colour' like lavender or brick red. If you tone from dark to medium to light and back again you cannot go wrong. Place your soft contrasts between motifs, not within them.

ZIGZAGS AND STEPS

To get away from the tennis match effect of rows of motifs typical of Fair Isle, I scratched around in my imagination for designs to carry the eye up and down the garment. The Zigzag and the larger Jack's Back were perfect simple-to-knit, two-colour-a-row solutions.

The little fleur-de-lys decorations at the corners are just enough to make the patterns less predictable as they bend their way up or across the garments in dark and light shadings. Even though they have only two colours in a row, if you introduce enough changes of colour you will create a rich complexity that belies the simple structure. The charts for the Zigzag and Jack's Back Stripe are also in *Glorious Knitting*.

Another variation on the stripe theme is my Step design. Step shapes are wonderfully rhythmic to knit. A few simple calculations can start you on one of the most structured of geometric vehicles for colour.

Having a very imprecise mind, I never bother to ensure that my steps maintain an ordered progression. I aim to get the first few rows of the pattern right and then let the structure flow organically, making a virtue of my mistakes.

ROMEO AND JULIET COAT

Of all the garments that Zoë Hunt and I have conjured up together, this remains a favourite. Watching a dress rehearsal of Nureyev's *Romeo and Juliet*, I was knocked sideways by the luxurious great sleeves on the costumes. The colours of the production were silvery greens and blues on one family, with deep rose maroons and reds on the other. These burnt reds in many shades and great drapes of fabric really captured my imagination in that theatre.

I soon inflamed Zoë with the idea of doing this huge coat based on those *Romeo and Juliet* costumes. She designed the shape of the body, and we both started on the sleeves together, I knitting one and she the other. Our first attempt had a great deal of man-made fibre, in the form of bulky but lightweight bouclé. This made it possible for the sleeves to be big without weighing as much as if made of natural fibres. We rarely use man-mades anymore, and this natural-fibre version does come out on the heavy side. If you do not have qualms about synthetics, you could do a lighter version by using a fluffy synthetic yarn for the big ridges in those massive sleeves.

This dramatic coat shape is also a superb structure for all sorts of schemes. I did the huge Map coat (page 71) like this, altering the sleeve to a kimono square. The map landscape extravaganza was a grateful response to a commission from the Aberdeen Art Gallery in Scotland. I had long been thrilled by the wild beauty of the northwest coast of Scotland and the Hebridean Islands, with their intensely beautiful hills of bracken and mossy stones, gushing streams and soft, magical light. I tried to sum up in a great coat all the impressions I had gathered since my first trip to Scotland in 1964. Since the coat is knitted in panels, it lends itself to mirror images. I could see huge brocade flowers done gorgeously in this shape.

Many colour schemes could be tried with the Romeo and Juliet coat design. After the original red version, which

Left: Romeo and Juliet coat with a dark version of the Persian Poppy waistcoat (page 75) against a wall of Virginia creeper on Hampstead Heath in North London.

35

appears in *Glorious Knitting*, we did a pastel version, mostly in cream with dots of pale blue, apricot and pink. Another variation, made for a lecturer in Yorkshire, uses tweedy browns and mosses and deep purply maroons (page 27).

The coat would also be very dramatic done in black, with very close tones of bottle green, purple, navy, and similar dark shades.

Zoë and I did do one version of the big-sleeved coat with an uninterrupted striped back, but I felt that the wide stripe running horizontally without a break was not as flattering as the broken, unmatched one in the pattern given here.

YARNS FOR ROMEO AND JULIET COAT

Average yarn weight used – chunky (bulky)
Rowan *Rowanspun Tweed* in the foll 4 colours:
    A (#753) cranberry – 700g (24½oz)
    B (#758) confetti – 100g (3½oz)
    C (#760) caviar – 200g (7oz)
    D (#756) one a.m. – 100g (3½oz)
Rowan *Classic Tweed* in the foll colour:
    E (#454) heather grey – 50g (1¾oz)
Rowan *Light Tweed* in the foll 3 colours:
    F (#216) cherrymix – 275g (10oz)
    G (#212) jungle – 50g (1¾oz)
    H (#221) Pacific – 25g (1oz)
Rowan *Lightweight DK* in the foll 8 colours:
    J (#90) bright jade – 25g (1oz)
    L (#55) medium blue – 25g (1oz)
    M (#501) hyacinth – 125g (4½oz)
    N (#94) grape – 225g (8oz)
    Q (#96) magenta – 150g (5½oz)
    R (#45) red – 150g (5½oz)
    S (#91) dark green – 50g (1¾oz)
    T (#72) gold – 25g (1oz)
Rowan *Silkstones* in the foll 4 colours:
    U (#826) chili – 150g (5½oz)
    W (#829) woad – 150g (5½oz)
    X (#830) mulled wine – 150g (5½oz)
    Y (#831) orchid – 150g (5½oz)
Rowan *Mohair* in the foll 4 colours:
    Z (#890) bronze – 150g (5½oz)
    a (#8346) rust – 150g (5½oz)
    b (#8776) maroon – 300g (11oz)
    c (#H6408) grape – 200g (7oz)

NEEDLES

One pair each of 5½mm (US size 9) and 6½mm (US size 10½) needles *or size to obtain correct tension (gauge)*
One 5½mm (US size 9) and one 6½mm (US size 10½) circular needle 100cm (39") long

SIZE AND MEASUREMENTS

One size to fit up to 91cm (36") bust
Actual width across back bodice below armhole shaping 47cm (18¾")
Actual width across back bodice at shoulders 33cm (13")
Length to shoulder 129cm (51¾")
Sleeve length 70cm (27½")

TENSION (GAUGE)

15 sts and 19 rows over st st stripe patt on 6½mm (US size 10½) needles
15½ sts and 18 rows to 10cm (4") over bodice colour patt on 6½mm (US size 10½) needles
Check your tension (gauge) before beginning.

NOTES

When working back bodice chart from 181st-192nd chart rows, carry only spot background colour (DW) across back of work between red outline (RRU) and use a separate length of each colour for all other areas. From 193rd-201st chart rows carry both spot background colour (DW) and circle outline colour (BH) across entire row, weaving them around working yarn on every 3rd st when not in use to keep bodice firm, and use a separate length of each colour for all other areas of colour. From 202nd chart row to end of chart use 2 separate bobbins of yarn for circle outline colour (BH), one on each side of central circles and cont working spot background colour across entire row as before. Work front bodices in the same way.
Read chart from right to left for RS (knit) rows and from left to right for WS (purl) rows.
Use 1 strand of yarn where there is only one letter to represent the colours, 2 strands of yarn where there are two letters and 3 strands of yarn where there are three letters, i.e. 'UXZ' means 1 strand each of U, X and Z.
When the coat is completed, fold and lay flat to store, because hanging it will stretch the knitted fabric.

BACK

The back is begun in 2 separate sections and joined below the armhole. After the 2 back sections are completed, the back bodice is then worked in one piece to the neck and shoulders. The lower edge of the coat is curved to make it hang correctly when worn.

LEFT BACK

Using 5½mm (US size 9) needles and A, cast on 88 sts.

Beg with a K row, work 7 rows in st st to form hem, so ending with a RS row.

Knit 1 row to form hemline.

Change to 6½mm (US size 10½) needles and, using Ac, cont as foll:

1st-8th rows Beg with a K row, work 8 rows in st st.*

Still using Ac and cont in st st, beg shaping curved edge as foll:

9th row (RS) K46, turn leaving rem 42 sts unworked on left-hand needle.

10th row and all foll WS rows Purl to end.

11th row K52, turn leaving rem 36 sts unworked.

13th row K58, turn leaving rem 30 sts unworked.

15th row K64, turn leaving rem 24 sts unworked.

17th row K70, turn leaving rem 18 sts unworked.

19th row K76, turn leaving rem 12 sts unworked.

21st row K82, turn leaving rem 6 sts unworked.

23rd row K all 88 sts.

24th row Purl to end.

This completes curved edge shaping.

Keeping centre back edge (beg of next row) straight, cont in st st, shaping side-seam edge (end of next row) by dec 1 st at end of next row, then dec 1 st at side seam edge on every foll 3rd row until 36 sts rem AND AT THE SAME TIME, work in stripes over next 154 rows as foll:

2 rows Cc, 4 rows CN, 4 rows FNX, 3 rows QQY, 2 rows FXZ, 1 row NRR, 3 rows UXZ, 3 rows EUX, 2 rows EGX, 2 rows GXb, 6 rows AX, 4 rows WXX, 3 rows MMY, 2 rows CYY, 3 rows Cb, 8 rows FFb, 2 rows FFN, 1 row MMY, 2 rows QQY, 2 rows NUY, 3 rows NUX, 2

rows NUZ, 6 rows UUZ, 3 rows FUU, 5 rows CFF, 5 rows FFN, 1 row YYY, 1 row QQY, 3 rows FRR, 1 row FGb, 1 row RRU, 2 rows FGb, 7 rows GXa, 2 rows GSS, 1 row GSX, 2 rows FGX, 4 rows AX, 3 rows FNX, 1 row QQY, 2 rows EXY, 3 rows GWX, 3 rows WXa, 1 row RXa, 3 rows NRR, 3 rows AW, 4 rows CF, 4 rows CX, 2 rows WXb, 3 rows NNR, 1 row RRU, 1 row QQU, 4 rows NUb, 1 row LLN, 1 row LNY, 2 rows EN, 2 rows Ea and 2 rows Aa.**

Leave these 36 sts on a spare needle.

RIGHT BACK

Work as for left back to *.

Still using Ac, beg shaping curved edge as foll:

9th row and all foll RS rows Knit to end.

10th row P46, turn leaving rem 42 sts unworked on left-hand needle.

12th row P52, turn leaving rem 36 sts unworked.

14th row P58, turn leaving rem 30 sts unworked.

16th row P64, turn leaving rem 24 sts unworked.

18th row P70, turn leaving rem 18 sts unworked.

20th row P76, turn leaving rem 12 sts unworked.

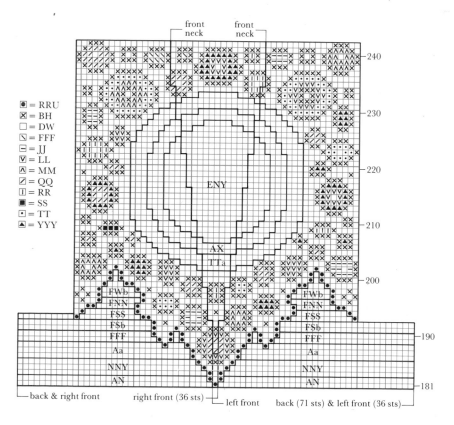

22nd row P82, turn leaving rem 6 sts unworked.

24th row Purl all 88 sts.

This completes curved edge shaping. Keeping centre back edge (end of next row) straight, cont in st st, shaping side-seam edge (beg of next row) by dec 1 st at beg of next row, then dec 1 st at side seam edge on every foll 3rd row until 36 sts rem AND AT THE SAME TIME, work in stripes over next 154 rows as for left back, but working stripes in reverse order of left back, so beg with 2 rows Aa and ending with 2 rows Cc.***

BODICE

Join left and right back tog on next row as foll:

179th row (RS) Using AN and with RS facing, K35 sts of right back, K tog last st of right back and first st of left back, K rem 35 sts of left back. 71 sts.

180th row Using AN, purl.

Beg with a K row, cont in st st foll chart from 181st chart row, until 192nd chart row has been completed, so ending with a WS row (see Notes for colourwork techniques).

ARMHOLE SHAPING

Keeping patt correct, cast (bind) off 10 sts at beg of next 2 rows. 51 sts.

Cont in patt until 242nd chart row has been completed.

Leave sts on a spare needle.

RIGHT FRONT

Work as for left back to **. 36 sts.

BODICE

179th-180th row Using AN, work 2 rows in st st.

Beg with a K row, cont in st st foll chart from 181st chart row (between chart markers for right front), until 186th chart row has been completed, so ending with a WS row.

NECK AND ARMHOLE SHAPING

Keeping patt correct throughout, dec 1 st at beg of next row (neck edge), then dec 1 st at neck edge on every 6th row 8 times more, AND AT THE SAME TIME when there are same number of rows as back to armhole, cast (bind) off 10 sts at armhole edge on next row.

When neck shaping has been completed, cont in patt on rem 17 sts until 242nd chart row has been completed.

Leave sts on a spare needle.

LEFT FRONT

Work as for right back to ***. 36 sts.

BODICE

179th-180th row Using AN, work 2 rows in st st.

Beg with a K row, cont in st st foll chart from 181st chart row (between chart markers for left front), until 186th chart row has been completed, so ending with a WS row.

NECK AND ARMHOLE SHAPING

Complete as for right front, reversing neck and armhole shaping.

LEFT SLEEVE

Using size 5½mm (US size 9) needles and AU, cast on 24 sts. Work in K1, P1 rib for 32 rows, shaping cuff by inc 1 st at each end of 7th row and then every foll 6th row until there are 34 sts AND AT THE SAME TIME work stripes as foll:

3 row AU, 2 rows AQ, 4 rows NNXX, 2 rows FFNU, 1 row FFNW, 3 rows CFW, 2 rows SSW, 3 rows CNW, 3 rows YYY, 2 rows YYb, 4 rows AFQ, 3 rows NQQ, so ending with a WS row. 34 sts.

Using 5½mm (US size 9) circular needle and AY, cont working back and forth in rows shaping sleeve as foll:

Next row (RS) *K2, make 1 st by picking up horizontal loop lying before next st and working into the back of it – called make 1 –, (K1, make 1) 3 times, rep from * 5 times more, (K1, make 1) 3 times, K1. 61 sts.

Purl 1 row.

Next row (K1, make 1) to last st, K1. 121 sts.

Purl 1 row.

Next row (K1, make 1, K1) to last st, K1. 181 sts.

Using SSW, purl 1 row.

Change to 6½mm (US size 10½) circular needle and work 92 rows without shaping in stripe patt, working stripes in st st and reverse st st alternately as foll:

Using Ac, K 1 row, (K 1 row, P 1 row)

twice; using YYY, P 1 row, K 1 row; using AFb, P 2 rows, (K1 row, P 1 row) twice; using RRUU, (P 1 row, K 1 row) twice; using FFNa, P 1 row, (P 1 row, K 1 row) twice; using QQQ, K 1 row; using MMM, P 1 row, K 1 row; using QQQ, P 1 row; using NYb, K 2 rows, (P 1 row, K 1 row) 3 times; using MYY, K 1 row, P 1 row, K 1 row; using AFZ, P 2 rows, K 1 row, P 1 row; using DWW, P 1 row, K 1 row, P 1 row; using Qab, K 2 rows, P 1 row; using CWW, P 1 row, K 1 row, P 1 row; using AFb, K 1 row, (K 1 row, P 1 row) 4 times; using RRUU, P 1 row, K 1 row, P 1 row; using FFYc, K 1 row, (K 1 row, P 1 row) twice; using MMM, P 1 row, K 1 row, P 1 row; using AFa, K 1 row, (K 1 row, P 1 row) 3 times; using NQQ, P 1 row, K 1 row, P 1 row; using RUUb, K 2 rows, P 1 row, K 1 row; using NNYY, K 1 row, P 1 row; using AZb, K 2 rows, (P 1 row, K 1 row) twice, so ending with a WS row.****

Using AZb, dec across next row as foll:
Next row (RS) K35, (K3 tog) 34 times, K44. 113 sts.
Change to 5½mm (US size 9) needles and using AFF, P 1 row, K 1 row, P 1 row. Cast (bind) off while working K35, (K2 tog) 17 times, K44.

RIGHT SLEEVE
Work as for left sleeve to ****.
Using AZb, dec across next row as foll:
Next row (RS) K44, (K3 tog) 34 times, K35. 113 sts.
Change to 5½mm (US size 9) needles and using AFF, P 1 row, K 1 row, P 1 row. Cast (bind) off while working K44, (K2 tog) 17 times, K35.

FRONT BANDS
Press all pieces lightly on WS with a warm iron over a damp cloth, omitting ribbing.
Using 6½mm (US size 10½) needles and DW, join right shoulder seam as foll:
Place RS of back and RS of right front tog and, with WS of front facing and points of both spare needles at shoulder edge, insert needle knitwise through first st of right front and first st of back and knit in

the usual way, knit 2nd st on each needle in the same way, pass first st over 2nd st and off right-hand needle, cast (bind) off each st in the same way to neck edge.
Join left shoulder seam in the same way, leaving rem 17 sts of back neck on spare needle. Using invisible seam, join centre back seam. Fold lower hem to WS along hemline and slipstitch in place.
Using 5½mm (US size 9) circular needle and AX and with RS facing, pick up and K196 sts evenly up right front edge (approx 4 sts for every 5 rows), K across 17 sts of back neck from spare needle and pick up and K196 sts down left front edge. 409 sts.
Work back and forth in rows as foll:
Purl 1 row. Change to A and knit 2 rows to form hemline. Beg with a K row, work 8 rows in st st. Cast (bind) off loosely.

FINISHING
Fold front bands to WS along hemline and slipstitch in place. Using backstitch, join cast (bound) off edge of sleeves to vertical edge of armholes, matching centre of top of sleeve to shoulder seam and join cast (bound) off armhole shaping to sides of sleeves. Note *Do not confuse right and left sleeve. There are more gathers at back of coat than front.*
Join side and sleeve seams, using backstitch for stripes and invisible seam for ribbing. Press seams and hems lightly on WS with a warm iron over a damp cloth, omitting ribbing.

Left: Detail of the medallion from the Romeo and Juliet coat. For a colour scheme with a sunny glow, you could work the coat all in shades of yellow with high pastels and grey touches, as in the yellow Star jacket (page 61).

STARS AND DIAMONDS

The crisp points of diamonds and stars make them a clear-cutting element in textile design. To my mind, these two angular motifs are among the liveliest of the geometric forms. Diamonds remind me of Sicilian and Turkish painted carts and merry-go-round decoration, while stars conjure up the Islamic world and my first impressions as an American child of bold stars and stripes.

Virtually every culture has brought out some different aspect of these themes. The joy of studying the world's many decorative moods is to find the one that best suits your needs. Islamic stars usually have an intricate structure which connects with other geometric forms. In medieval France and England gold stars were often scattered on a blue painted ceiling – a motif also used on some enamelled boxes. Irish and American patchwork quilts give us several classic stars in joyously patterned fabrics.

Diamonds can be seen on figures of Harlequins, argyll knitting and backgammon boards, all of which give classic arrangements in which to display any colours we fancy. Tumbling Boxes is an intriguing use of diamonds which I always enjoy playing with. The way it changes from boxes to stars and back is quite fascinating.

I often knit each diamond of the boxes

Left: The Geometric Star cushion on a handsome tumbling-box quilt, with Victorian sewing delights from the textile collection at the V&A.

in a solid colour. But the pattern could be approached like the patchwork quilts that inspired it, with some of the diamonds worked in intricate patterns like the prints used in patchwork.

Outlined stars, like the ones on my waistcoat (page 57), are fun to knit. The yellow version (page 61) became the cover of the American edition of *Glorious* *Knitting* and proved so popular that Rowan has produced it in kit form. Most of my star patterns have the stars arranged in very symmetrical rows, but a gorgeously lively design could be made by using stars of constantly changing scale crammed together like a version of the Cross Patch coat (page 98). You could draw the stars on graph paper to

help you to concentrate on colour changing as you knit. I feel it is best to be instinctive about colour rather than planning it too carefully beforehand.

GEOMETRIC STAR CUSHION

In an antique market in London I came across a volume of Japanese textiles arranged by motifs. The star section contained this stunning design of a brocade. The text was in Japanese and the colours in black and white, so I was blissfully ignorant enough to do what I liked with the inspiration. I first tried a knitted version (page 56) of the design and then this stitched cushion.

One great advantage of needlepoint as a design medium is that you can fairly easily work out a design 'on the needle', as I like to, moving over the canvas in any direction. Working on the needle is more difficult in knitting, where you have to build up the design row by row. So you may like to try a geometric design like this one on canvas first and then chart it on graph paper and use it as a pattern for knitting.

Do add more colours to this cushion if you decide to make it. Since it is worked on a 7-mesh canvas with two strands of yarn, you can stitch this quickly, then try a different colour scheme which contrasts or tones with this one to make an interesting pair of cushions.

Having used this design as a jacket and cushion, you could go on to use it in all sorts of other ways. You could work it on 10-mesh canvas with single yarn, to make some handsome placemats, or a lampshade or chair covering. It could be expanded to make a carpet in softer colours – say greys and other stone colours.

Both Japanese and Islamic cultures are jam-packed with an astounding richness of geometric patterns just waiting to be brought to life by the textile colourist. We are lucky to have many books on the market that simplify these patterns for us, making them accessible to anyone interested in striking and original patterns as vehicles for unique colour schemes.

MATERIALS FOR GEOMETRIC STAR CUSHION

Rowan *Lightweight DK* in the following 14 colours and approximate amounts (each 25g ball contains approximately 67.5m or 74yd):

▨	91 (46m/50yd)	▨	501 (42m/45yd)
▨	89 (39m/42yd)	▨	127 (48m/52yd)
▨	90 (72m/78yd)	▨	121 (34m/37yd)
▨	125 (54m/59yd)	▨	57 (77m/84yd)
▨	63 (61m/66yd)	▨	53 (77m/84yd)
▨	95 (12m/13yd)	▨	605 (23m/25yd)
▨	96 (14m/15yd)	▨	106 (34m/37yd)

7-mesh double-thread or interlocked canvas 60cm (23½″) by 62cm (24¼″)
70cm (¾yd) of 90cm (36″) wide backing fabric and matching thread
38cm (15″) zipper
2.1m (2¼yd) of cord for edging
Finished needlepoint measures approximately 50cm (19½″) by 52cm (20¼″)

WORKING GEOMETRIC STAR CUSHION

The chart is 137 stitches wide by 142 stitches high. Count the canvas threads to mark the outline of the needlepoint onto the canvas. Make a paper template of the canvas outline and set aside to use later to block the finished needlepoint. Following the chart, work the embroidery in tent stitch using *two strands* of

Below: Looking at Islamic pots and tiles of turquoise and rich blues in the V&A led to the colour scheme for these richly coloured stars.

Lightweight DK together. Block the finished needlepoint by dampening it on the wrong side, pinning it out to the correct size following the paper template and leaving it to dry. Trim the canvas around the needlepoint. Cut the lining to the same size as the finished needlepoint plus 1.5cm (½″) extra all around for the seam allowance, after having inserted the zipper in the centre. With the right sides facing, sew the lining to the needlepoint and turn right side out. Press seams lightly with needlepoint face down. Sew cord around edge of needlepoint along seam.

IN SEARCH OF DIAMONDS AND STARS

A good exercise to awaken your perception of the world's cornucopia of decoration is to look for themes such as diamonds or stars or other basic motifs in as many disparate cultures as possible.

Think of Norwegian knitted garments using bold stars, Sicilian painted wagons using diamond borders and sunbursts of sharp diamond shapes, African woven diamonds in contrasting colours, and the wealth of Japanese and Islamic brocades using an extraordinary variety of stars. Having been raised in a polyglot society, I was exposed to all these influences. It was nothing for me to mix Chinese decorative motifs with Russian or American Indian ones and so discover the joyous connections between these scattered cultures in their use of geometric forms.

These forms, of course, are only empty vessels to be filled with rich blendings of colour. They are often oversimplified when we spot them, waiting for us textile interpreters to add that personal magic element of uplifting colour. I invented my Big Diamond design to give a long line to a full jacket, and the Outlined Stars arose from my fascination with Islam's interwoven geometric structures.

Argyll or harlequin diamonds are ideal structures for colour. We often see them in limited colours because of commercial considerations, but I myself love to pack them with copious blends of

colour and slightly varied textures.

Since the design progression of harlequin diamonds is quickly memorized by the knitter, one's concentration can be focused on the colour blendings. And because each yarn is worked in place, intarsia-style, there is no reason not to have different colours or tones in each section of the design. You will notice that I often work my diamonds in close

Opposite page: The plain Diamond shape and its offshoot, the Houses shape, are jaunty structures for building colours into design.

Top and middle left: The Big Diamond jacket in dark colours.

Bottom left: Lurex variation of Brick Diamond pattern (see page 50) in ancient Byzantine tones.

*This page: Big
Diamond jacket from
'Glorious Knitting',
in a bright colour
scheme (above). The
Pyramid of Fruit
jacket (above right).
I was drawn to the
lively pendants in this
Indian painting
(below).*

*Opposite page:
Cotton and silk Big
Diamond tunic in
Picasso circus colours.*

antiqued tones, but the examples we have found in the V&A show us a lively, more contrasting palette.

A development from the diamond shape is my Houses pattern. I first used this as a border in several sweaters and cushion covers after seeing it used in Greek and Turkish textiles. I dubbed it Houses, because it reminds me of those jolly rows of gaily painted beach houses at the English seaside. When you pile them up row after row in an allover pattern, using lots of different colours, they really make a rich display.

Looking at the ceramic Harlequin figures in the V&A makes me itch to do little rows of brightly coloured diamonds. You could take exactly the

colours shown, plus several more complementary tones, and knit some wonderful crewnecks for children or adults, even adding the ruffle at the neck.

BRICK DIAMOND V-NECK

When I first came to London in those far-off Sixties, there was just one colour in the urban landscape that I did not like: that dusty ochre kind of brick used for so many nineteenth-century buildings. However they may have looked when new, after a century or so of air pollution these walls had turned a dismal non-colour, especially drab and sad in the grey light.

Then one day I took a close, lingering look at a typically grimy example, and it was as if I was seeing it for the first time! There was an intense world of colour waiting to be perceived. Grape purples, flame blues, rusts, plums and endless shades of ochre and camel were just a few of the smouldering shades lurking in those walls. I sat down and knitted every colour I could find a yarn for into the classic argyll diamonds of the Brick Diamond sweater.

If you want to have a go, just gather at least twenty light tones and twenty darker ones. For the richest effect choose mohairs, wools, bouclés, silks and tweed yarns and make tweedy 'marls' by knitting two yarns together. Steer clear of anything close to clean white, keeping the lightest colour a deep beige and the darkest a gunmetal grey.

YARNS FOR BRICK DIAMOND V-NECK

Average yarn weight used – chunky (bulky)
Approx 450g (16oz) in a mixture of yarns and colours in dark shades A
Approx 450g (16oz) in a mixture of yarns and colours in light shades B

NEEDLES

One pair each of 5mm (US size 8) and 6mm (US size 10) needles *or size to obtain correct tension (gauge)*
One 5mm (US size 8) circular needle 40cm (15½″) long

SIZES AND MEASUREMENTS

One size to fit up to 107cm (42″) bust or chest
Actual width across back 58cm (23¼″)
Length to shoulder 61cm (24″)
Sleeve length to underarm 50cm (19¾″)

TENSION (GAUGE)

14 sts and 20 rows to 10cm (4″) over colour patt on 6mm (US size 10) needles
Check your tension (gauge) before beginning.

NOTES

When working colour patt, do not carry yarn across back of work, but use a separate length of each colour for each diamond, twisting yarns when changing colours to avoid holes.
Before beginning, group dark shades (A) and light shades (B) into two separate piles.
Read chart from right to left for RS (knit) rows and from left to right for WS (purl) rows.

BACK

*Using 5mm (US size 8) needles and A, cast on 73 sts.
Beg K1, P1 rib as foll:
<u>1st rib row</u> (RS) K1, (P1, K1) to end.
<u>2nd rib row</u> P1, (K1, P1) to end.
Last 2 rows form rib patt. Work 11 rows more in rib patt in stripes of random shades of A and B, so ending with a RS row.
<u>Next row</u> (inc row) Using same colour as last row, rib 5, make 1 st by picking up horizontal loop lying before next st and working into the back of it – called make 1 –, (rib 9, make 1) 7 times, rib 5. 81 sts.
Change to 6mm (US size 10) needles and beg with a K row, work in st st foll chart from first chart row for diamond patt, working each diamond in different colours and in random stripes, until 29th chart row has been completed. Cont in colour patt rep 2nd-29th chart rows until back measures 36cm (14″) from beg, ending with a WS row.

ARMHOLE SHAPING

Keeping patt correct, cast (bind) off 8 sts at beg of next 2 rows. 65 sts.*
Cont in patt without shaping until armhole measures 25cm (10″), ending with a WS row.

SHOULDER SHAPING

Keeping patt correct cast (bind) off 6 sts at beg of next 2 rows and 7 sts at beg of next 4 rows.
Slip rem 25 sts onto spare needle for back neck to be used later for neckband.

FRONT

Work as for back from * to *, using same colours as for back.
Cont in patt without shaping until armhole measures 6cm (2½″), ending with a WS row.

NECK SHAPING

Beg neck shaping by dividing for neck on next row as foll:
<u>Next row</u> (RS) Patt 32 sts, cast (bind) off

next st (centre st), patt to end. 32 sts at each side of neck.

Next row Patt to last 2 sts before neck edge, P2 tog, slip rem sts (left shoulder) onto a spare needle (see foll Note).

Note *If desired, work both sides of neck at same time with separate balls of yarn.*

RIGHT NECK AND SHOULDER EDGES
Keeping patt correct, work 2 rows without shaping. Dec 1 st at neck edge on next row and then on every 3rd row until 20 sts rem. Work without shaping until there are same number of rows as back to shoulder, ending at armhole edge. Cast (bind) off 6 sts at beg of next row, then cast (bind) off 7 sts at beg of foll alternate row. Work 1 row without shaping. Cast (bind) off rem sts.

LEFT NECK AND SHOULDER EDGES
With WS facing, rejoin yarn at neck edge to sts at other side of neck and P2 tog,

work in patt to end.
Complete as for right neck and shoulder edges from ** to **.

SLEEVES

Note *If desired, work both sleeves at same time with separate balls of yarn.*

Using 5mm (US size 8) needles and same colour as cast on for back, cast on 33 sts. Work in K1, P1 rib patt as for back using same colours as back until 13 rib rows have been completed, so ending with a RS row.

Next row (inc row) Rib 4, make 1, (rib 5, make 1) 5 times, rib 4. 39 sts.

Change to 6mm (US size 10) needles and beg with a K row, work in st st foll chart from first chart row, rep 2nd-29th chart rows and using same colours as back for diamonds, but in reverse order from neck downwards, AND AT THE SAME TIME shape sleeve by inc 1 st at each end of every 5th row until there are 71 sts.

Work in patt without shaping until sleeve measures 55cm (21½″) from beg or required length.

Cast (bind) off loosely.

NECKBAND

Press all pieces lightly on WS with a warm iron over a damp cloth, omitting ribbing.

Using backstitch, join shoulder seams.

Using 5mm (US size 8) circular needle and same colour as 9th row of back ribbing and with RS facing, beg at left shoulder seam and pick up and K38 sts

⊠ = A
☐ = B

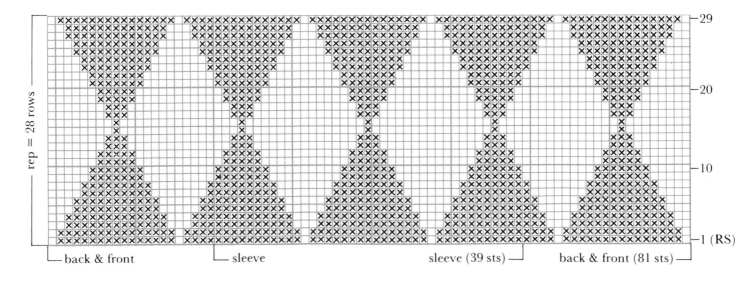

rep = 28 rows

29

20

10

1 (RS)

└ back & front ┘   └ sleeve ┘   └ sleeve (39 sts) ┘   └ back & front (81 sts) ┘

evenly down left front neck, 2 sts in centre front neck st, 38 sts evenly up right front neck, K25 sts of back neck from spare needle. 103 sts.

Beg K1, P1 rib as foll:

<u>1st round</u> Using same colour as 8th row of back rib, P1, (K1, P1) 18 times, sl 1-K1-psso (centre front reached), K2 tog, (P1, K1) to end of round.

<u>2nd round</u> Using same colour as 7th row of back rib, rib to centre 4 sts of front neck, sl 1-K1-psso, K2 tog, rib to end.

Rep last round 6 times more, using same colours as back rib from 6th to first rows. Using same colour as back cast-on, cast (bind) off loosely in rib, working decs at centre front as before.

FINISHING

Using backstitch, join cast (bound) off edge of sleeves to vertical edge of arm-holes, matching centre of top of sleeve to shoulder seam, and join cast (bound) off armhole shaping to sides of sleeves.

Join side and sleeve seams, using back-stitch for st st and invisible seam for rib. Press seams lightly on WS with a warm iron over a damp cloth, omitting ribbing.

GEOMETRIC STAR JACKET

This is a real show-off piece! Done in so many colours and intricate patterns, it looks totally daunting to all but the most expert knitter. In fact, each section of the pattern has only two colours per row within its area, and the large stars have a definite rhythm that makes them a joy to knit. You could say it is simply an ex-panded argyll pattern.

The striking star shapes are as the original in a Japanese fabric book, but I reworked the little two-colour patterns to make them easy to knit. Having been strolling through the V & A collection of Islamic blue and green pottery, I found the rich colour there an inspired choice for this design. These vessels glow in their pure pools of colour, encouraging us to reach for clean, deep tones of yarn. But if ever there was a pattern in which to go mad on the colours, this is it! Do try your own interpretations.

YARNS FOR GEOMETRIC STAR JACKET

Average yarn weight used – 2 strands of light-weight double knitting (sport) or 1 strand of chunky (bulky)

Rowan *Rowanspun Tweed* in the foll colour:

A (#756) one a.m. – 200g (7oz)

Rowan *Lightweight DK* in the foll 16 colours:

B (#57) dark blue – 225g (8oz)
C (#127) purple – 75g (2¾oz)
D (#55) medium blue – 100g (3½oz)
E (#90) bright jade – 150g (5½oz)
F (#501) hyacinth – 75g (2¾oz)
G (#53) airforce – 75g (2¾oz)
H (#50) cornflower – 50g (1¾oz)
I (#100) deep jade – 75g (2¾oz)
J (#125) turquoise – 100g (3½oz)
L (#99) dark grape – 100g (3½oz)
M (#106) dark olive – 50g (1¾oz)
N (#121) lilac – 75g (2¾oz)
Q (#124) emerald – 75g (2¾oz)
R (#91) dark green – 75g (2¾oz)
S (#63) powder blue – 25g (1oz)
T (#89) pale jade – 50g (1¾oz)

Rowan *Botany* in the foll colour:

U (#635) taupe – 50g (1¾oz)

Rowan *Light Tweed* in the foll 2 colours:

V (#221) Pacific – 75g (2¾oz)
Z (#220) jade – 75g (2¾oz)

NEEDLES AND NOTIONS

One pair each of 5½mm (US size 9) and 6mm (US size 10) needles *or size to obtain correct tension (gauge)*

One 5½mm (US size 9) circular needle 100cm (39") long

5 buttons

SIZE AND MEASUREMENTS

One size to fit up to 117cm (46") bust or chest

Actual width across back at underarm 75cm (30")

Length to shoulder 68cm (27")

Sleeve length 42cm (16½")

TENSION (GAUGE)

18 sts and 20 rows to 10cm (4") over colour patt on 6mm (US size 10) needles

Check your tension (gauge) before beginning.

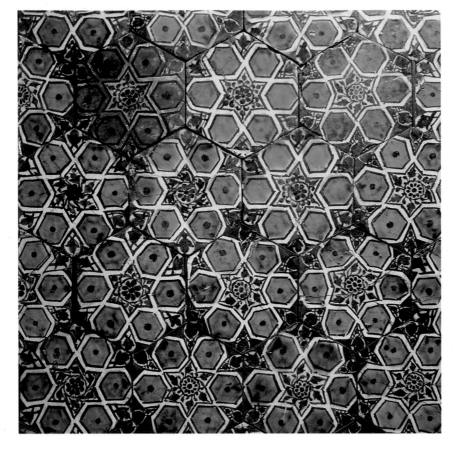

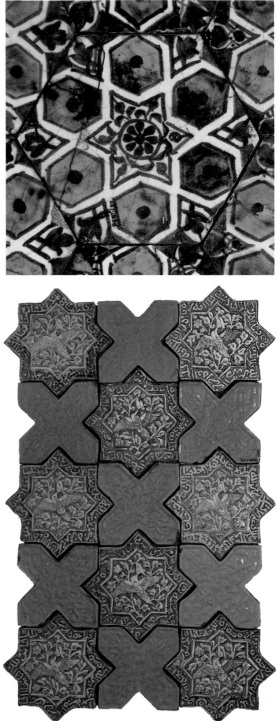

This page: Islamic star tiles inspire us to use rich pools of colour.

Opposite page: The eighteenth-century velvet and brocade quilt embroidered with gold and silver and the delightfully coloured Harlequin figures from the V&A should get any designer going.

NOTES

Use a separate length of each colour for each star and hexagon, twisting yarns when changing colours to avoid holes. Carry star and hexagon colours only across back of each individual star or hexagon, weaving colour not in use around working yarn.

Read chart from right to left for RS (knit) rows and from left to right for WS (purl) rows.

Use 1 strand of yarn where there is only one letter to represent the colour, 2 strands of yarn where there are two letters and 3 strands of yarn where there are three letters, i.e. 'ZZZ' means 3 strands of Z.

The colour sequence table must be read in conjunction with 'map' diagram for colours used.

BACK

Using 5½mm (US size 9) needles and A, cast on 113 sts.
*Beg K1, P1 rib as foll:
1st rib row (RS) Using A, K1, (P1, K1) to end.
2nd rib row Using A, P1, (K1, P1) to end.
First and 2nd rows form rib patt.
Work 17 rows more in rib patt in stripes as foll:
3 rows BB, 1 row CC, 1 row A, 2 rows UUU, 1 row A, 1 row BB, 1 row DD, 3 rows EE, 1 row FF, 2 rows BB, 1 row A, so ending with a RS row.*

Next row (inc row) Using A, rib 4, make 1 st by picking up horizontal loop lying before next st and working into the back of it – called make 1 –, (rib 5, make 1) 21 times, rib 4. 135 sts.

Change to 6mm (US size 10) needles and beg with a K row, work in st st foll chart from first chart row for stars and hexagons and foll colour sequence table and

'map' diagram for colours, until 116th chart row has been completed, so ending with a WS row (see Notes for reading chart).

NECK SHAPING

Divide for neck on next row as foll:

117th chart row (RS) Patt 61 sts, cast (bind) off centre 13 sts, patt to end.

118th chart row Patt to neck edge, slip rem sts (right shoulder) onto a spare needle (see foll Note). 61 sts at each side of neck.

Note *If desired work both sides of neck at same time with separate balls of yarn.*

LEFT NECK EDGE

Keeping patt correct throughout, cast (bind) off 7 sts at beg of next row (neck edge). 54 sts. Work one row without shaping. Cast (bind) off.

RIGHT NECK EDGE

With WS facing, rejoin yarn to neck edge of sts at other side of neck and cast (bind) off 7 sts, patt to end. Work 2 rows without shaping. Cast (bind) off.

Overleaf: Luminous blue and green Persian pots from the V&A, sitting on the Blue Patch crewneck and the Geometric Star jacket and cushion.

53

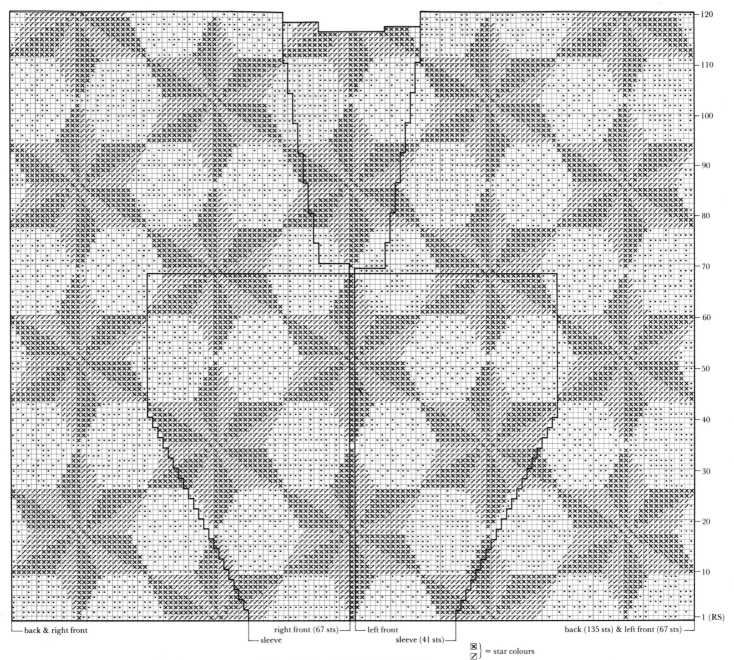

back & right front
sleeve
right front (67 sts)
left front
sleeve (41 sts)
back (135 sts) & left front (67 sts)

⊠
⊠ } = star colours

⊡
☐ } = hexagon colours

NOTE see colour
sequence table and
diagram for actual colours.

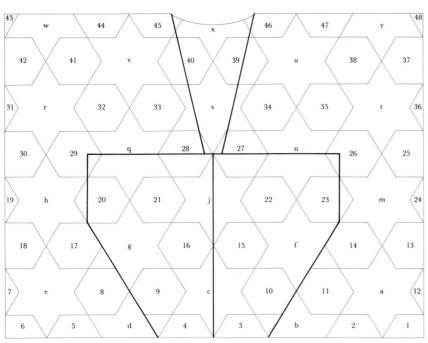

RIGHT FRONT

<u>Note</u> *If desired, work both fronts at same time
with separate balls of yarn. The fronts of the
jacket in the photo are a mirror image of the
instructions given here.*

*(Due to lack of space, the charts of the back and
fronts had to be combined, thereby reversing the
fronts.)*

**Using 5½mm (US size 9) needles and
A, cast on 57 sts.

Work as for back from * to *.

<u>Next row</u> (inc row) Using A, rib 2, make
1, (rib 6, make 1) 9 times, rib 1. 67 sts.

Change to 6mm (US size 10) needles and
beg with a K row, work in st st foll chart

58

COLOUR SEQUENCE

Hexagon	•	□	Hexagon	•	□	Star	☒	◪
1	GG	CC	28	DD	VVV	d	LL	CC
2	BB	EE	29	FF	NN	e	BB	EE
3	GG	ZZZ	30	LL	DD	f	BB	DD
4	UUU	DD	31	FF	EE	g	RR	DD
5	GG	VVZ	32	RR	SS	h	II	VVV
6	A	MZZ	33	GG	EE	j	LL	EE
7	UUU	DD	34	A	CC	m	QQ	JJ
8	FF	ZZZ	35	QQ	VVV	n	RR	TT
9	A	VVV	36	A	EE	q	A	JJ
10	EE	NN	37	RR	MV	r	QQ	TT
11	MM	GG	38	UUU	NN	s	BB	HH
12	UUU	II	39	RR	ZZZ	t	BB	FF
13	FF	VVV	40	A	EE	u	LL	JJ
14	UUU	CC	41	MM	HH	v	BB	DD
15	QQ	HH	42	RR	JJ	w*	A	EE
16	FF	NN	43	UUU	DD	x	GG	FF
17	A	CC	44	FF	ZZZ	y*	GG	EE
18	LL	MM	45	A	VVV			
19	EE	SS	46	EE	NN			
20	UUU	EZ	47	GG	MM			
21	GG	CC	48	UUU	RR			
22	FF	ZZZ						
23	A	UUU						
24	GG	TT	Star	☒	◪			
25	DD	ZZZ	a	A	HH			
26	LL	EE	b	II	VVV			
27	GG	MM	c	A	JJ			

NOTE Where there are 2 or 3 letters, 2 or 3 strands of yarn are used, i.e. 'VVV' means 3 strands of V. See diagram for positions of Hexagons and Stars. *To match Stars at shoulders reverse colours for w and y on front.

from first chart row (between markers for front) for stars and hexagons and foll colour sequence table and 'map' diagram for colours **, until 70th chart row has been completed, so ending with a WS row.

NECK SHAPING
Keeping patt correct throughout, cast (bind) off 6 sts at beg of next row (neck edge). 61 sts.
Work 3 rows without shaping.
***Dec 1 st at neck edge on next row, then on every foll 6th row 6 times more. 54 sts.
Work 9 rows without shaping.
Cast (bind) off loosely.***

LEFT FRONT
Work as for right front from ** to **, until 69th chart row has been completed, so ending with a RS row.

NECK SHAPING
Keeping patt correct throughout, cast (bind) off 6 sts at beg of next row (neck edge). 61 sts.
Work 4 rows without shaping. Complete as for right front from *** to ***.

SLEEVES
Note *If desired, work both sleeves at same time with separate balls of yarn.*
Using 5½mm (US size 9) needles and A, cast on 33 sts.
Work 19 rows in rib as for back, so ending with a RS row.
Next row (inc row) Using A, rib 2, make 1, (rib 4, make 1) 7 times, rib 3. 41 sts.
Change to 6mm (US size 10) needles and beg with a K row, work in st st foll chart from first chart row (between chart markers for sleeve) until 41st chart row has been completed, AND AT THE SAME

Pages 56 and 57: Star waistcoat from 'Glorious Knitting' and the Geometric Star jacket, singing in Hampstead willow herb.

Above: Why not try a really over-the-top colour scheme for this design, using reds, blacks, golds, magentas, plus all the blues here and anything else that looks jolly?

Opposite page: Yellow Star jacket photographed in Malta and now available as a kit (top). The original Star jacket (middle). Grey Star jacket kit with English seaside beach huts (bottom).

TIME shape sleeve by inc 1 st at each end of 3rd row, then every foll alternate row until there are 81 sts.

Work without shaping until 68th chart row has been completed or until sleeve is required length.

Cast (bind) off loosely.

BUTTON BAND

Press all pieces lightly on WS with a warm iron over a damp cloth, omitting ribbing.

Using 5½mm (US size 9) needles and A and with RS facing, pick up and K74 sts evenly along centre edge of left front (or right front for man's version) between lower edge and beg of neck shaping.

Using A throughout, purl 1 row. Knit 3 rows to form hemline.

Beg with a P row, work in st st for 6 rows more.

Cast (bind) off loosely.

BUTTONHOLE BAND

Using 5½mm (US size 9) needles and A and with RS facing, pick up and K74 sts evenly along centre edge of right front (or left front for man's version) as for button

band, working buttonholes at same time as foll:

Pick up and K4 sts, *pick up and cast (bind) off next 2 sts, pick up and K14 sts including st already on needle, rep from * 3 times more, pick up and cast (bind) off next 2 sts, pick up and K4 sts including st already on needle.

Using A throughout, purl 1 row, casting on 2 sts over those cast (bound) off in last row.

Knit 3 rows to form hemline.

Work buttonholes on next 2 rows as foll:

<u>Next row</u> (WS) P4, *cast (bind) off 2 sts, P14 including st already on needle, rep from * 3 times more, cast (bind) off 2 sts, P4 including st already on needle.

<u>Next row</u> Knit, casting on 2 sts over those cast (bound) off in last row.

Work 4 rows more in st st.

Cast (bind) off loosely.

RIGHT FRONT POCKET

Using 5½mm (US size 9) needles and BB and with RS facing, pick up and K30 sts evenly along right side-seam edge of back between 12th and 45th chart rows (approx 5 sts for every 6 row ends).

Using BB throughout, purl 1 row.

Cast on 6 sts at beg of next row and knit across row. 36 sts.

****Cont in st st, dec 1 st at top edge of pocket on next row, then dec 1 st at same edge on every alternate row until 22 sts rem.

Cast (bind) off loosely.****

LEFT FRONT POCKET

Using 5½mm (US size 9) needles and BB and with RS facing, pick up and K30 sts evenly along left side-seam edge of back as for right front pocket.

Cast on 6 sts at beg of next row and purl across row. 36 sts.

Complete as for right front pocket from **** to ****.

POCKET BANDS

Using 5½mm (US size 9) needles and BB and with RS facing, pick up and K30 sts evenly along right front side-seam edge at position corresponding with pocket.

Using BB throughout, knit 1 row to form hemline. Beg with a K row, work in st st for 4 rows more. Cast (bind) off loosely. Work pocket band on left front in the same way.

COLLAR

Using 5½mm (US size 9) circular needle and A, cast on 181 sts.
Working back and forth in rows, work 11 rows in rib patt as for back in stripes as foll:
2 rows A, 2 rows BB, 1 row FF, 3 rows EE, 1 row DD, 1 row BB and 1 row A.

COLLAR SHAPING

Keeping rib patt correct, cast (bind) off 4 sts at beg of next 22 rows, then 6 sts at beg of next row 10 rows, AND AT THE SAME TIME work in stripes as foll:
2 rows UUU, 1 row A, 1 row CC, 3 rows BB, 2 rows JJ, 1 row TT, 3 rows GG, 1 row TT, 1 row NN, 3 rows DD, 1 row SS, 2 rows II, 1 row MM, 1 row GG, 2 rows EE, 1 row LL, 2 rows JJ, 1 row LL, 3 rows HH. Using HH, cast (bind) off rem 33 sts in rib.

FINISHING

Using backstitch, join shoulder seams. Mark back and front at side edges 22cm (9″) from shoulder seam. Using backstitch, join cast (bound) off edge of sleeves to back and front between markers, matching centre of top of sleeve to shoulder seam.
Fold pocket bands to WS of fronts along hemline and slipstitch in place. Slipstitch pocket linings to WS of fronts.
Join side and sleeve seams, using backstitch for st st and invisible seam for rib. Using backstitch, join shaped edge of collar to shaped edge of fronts and back neck. Fold buttonhole and button bands to WS along hemlines and slipstitch in place. Slipstitch collar ends to cast (bound) off edges of front neck shaping and front bands. Press seams lightly on WS with a warm iron over a damp cloth, omitting ribbing. Sew on buttons to correspond with buttonholes. Neaten buttonholes if desired by sewing inside and outside loosely together.

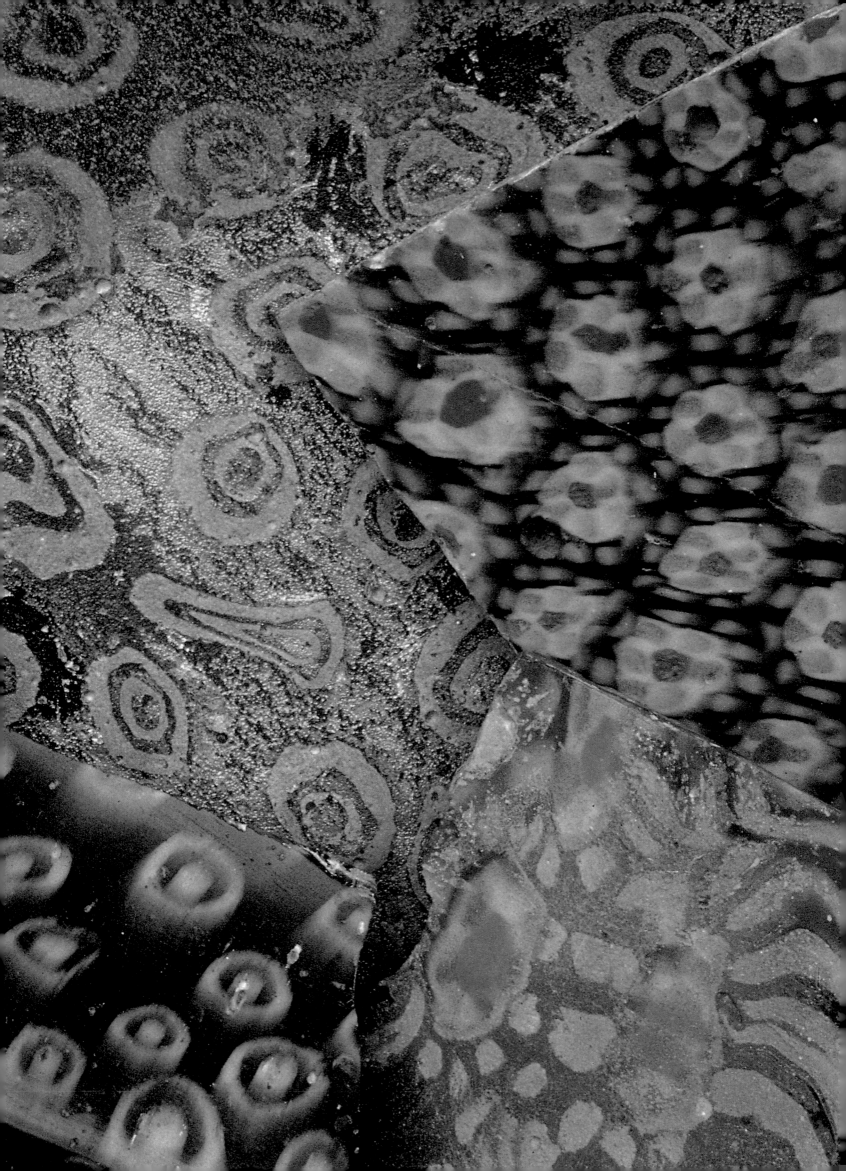

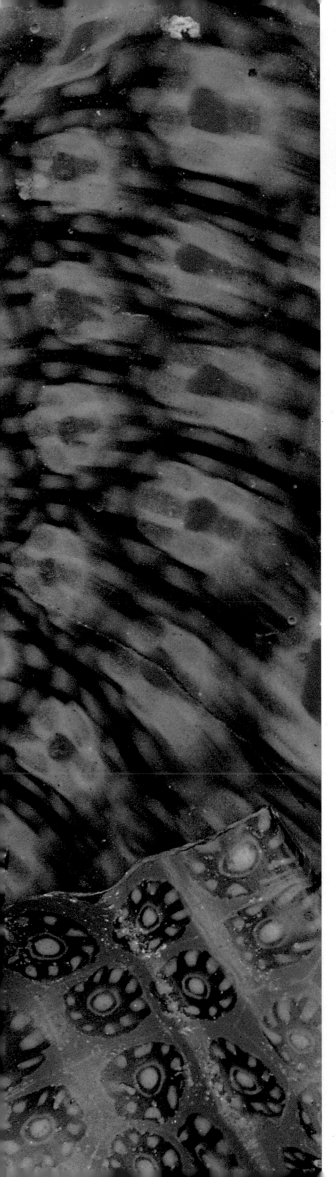

SPOTS AND DOTS

Maybe it started with spots made by raindrops on dark roads, or the scattering of seeds from a burst pod, or the dazzling variety of spots on animals, birds and insects – wherever the idea was born, men and women from time immemorial have decorated everything from themselves to their surroundings with playful arrangements of dots.

This motif pops up in all sorts of guises – for example, the embossed dots on Etruscan jewellery; the clusters of French knots in some embroideries, sometimes densely packed in one area, then gradually dispersing; and the classic polka dot pattern found in women's fashions and men's neckties.

I find my spots and dots design sources in many places. Speckled eggs are a great favourite. And, of course, the more intricate structures of glass paperweights have fascinated me so much that I used one as the inspiration for my first needlepoint. Also, for years I have dragged people to peer into the cases of Roman glass at the V&A. These fragments have the joyful exuberance of pretty candies embedded in glass.

On a larger scale the spot or dot becomes a circle. Circles have been a passion of mine ever since I first saw dots on a clown costume. I love the way different cultures handle this very playful theme. Often circles are the centre of the

Left: Fragments of Roman glass, showing subtle variations in scale. I particularly like the brown ground with black and white spots.

63

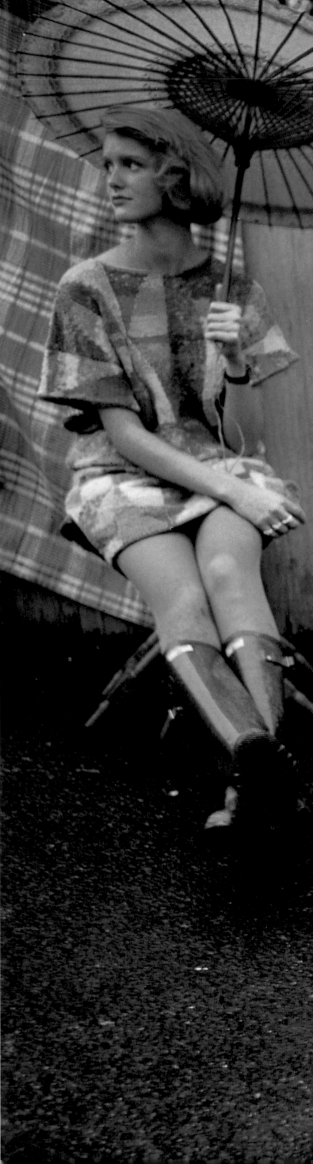

*Right: Cotton and
silk Diamond dress
(from 'Glorious
Knitting') and
Roman Glass
waistcoat
photographed on a
rainy day in London.*

*Below: Roman Glass
waistcoat, with its
explosion of spots and
dots.*

most elegant and sophisticated designs in carpets or Indian Tantric works of art.

ROMAN GLASS WAISTCOAT

The Romans were not the first people to use sprinkles of spots and dots, but surely they refined these candy-like motifs in their glassware to a fine art. The colour the glassmakers achieved so many years ago really moves me, particularly the elegant browns and off-teal blues.

For my Roman Glass waistcoat I took my cue from the random floating quality of the glass design arrangement and from every colour that was suggested, particularly the wonderful subtleties that occur through aging.

This sort of knitting is far easier to achieve than it appears. It is certainly far easier to knit than it is to draw a design on graph paper and try to follow it. The trick is to knit some dot or spot into every possible space of your design, while trying wherever possible not to let the motifs touch or line up in exact rows. I stripe the background with many changes of close colours and carry the outline and dot

colour across each row. The local jewel colours are knitted intarsia-style in the area or motif that contains them, so you have manageable lengths of each colour hanging down across the row, ready to be knitted in one small area. The only other complexity is changing the background colour in a few places to break things up a bit and at the same time change dot colour just within that background area.

LEOPARD SHAWL

One of my good customers once brought me a piece of leopard fur to copy as a knitted jacket. At first I was not at all sure if I could, or even wanted to, attempt it. After living with the pelt itself for a few days, I became aware of so many colours and subtle tones that I felt compelled to have a go. The results

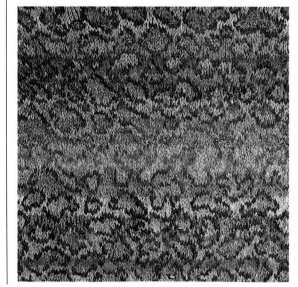

Top right: Pots suggesting animal markings, sitting on the Leopard shawl.

Bottom right: Detail of Leopard shawl.

Far right: The Leopard shawl and the Brick Diamond V-neck.

Left: Pictured here among other circular themes are a glass paperweight, Chinese stone snuff bottles, the knitted Map coat commissioned by the Aberdeen Art Gallery and the pale green Floating Circle crewneck (lower right-hand corner).

amazed me, and long after I completed the original jacket, I worked the same leopard spots on the shawl from memory.

I have used about fourteen browns and lavender-blues for outlines, twenty-one greys, dull yellows and beiges for the background, and sixteen beige-pinks, ochres and pale yellows for the centres of the spots. Wool bouclés, mohair, silk and some odd mixtures of synthetics and wool were used for texture. The fringe uses several shades of beige and grey wool yarns.

DESIGNING SPOT MOTIFS

The Persian Poppy (pages 74 and 75) is one of my classic early designs which I am endlessly feeding new colourings into. I dreamed it up as a constantly varying design to be knitted by Beatrice Bellini's knitters for her shop in London. I instructed the knitters to tie twenty colours together in varying lengths for the poppies and another twenty for the background, so that the same colours would always be appearing in a different order and proportion. The great advantage of this pattern is that you can take just two balls of yarn (containing as many joined colours as you can muster) off on your travels and be knitting a blaze of colour without having to drag along a laundry bag of yarn. The Persian Poppy instructions for this random effect appear in *Glorious Knitting*; here I give you a new colour scheme (page 74).

Other repeated circular motifs I have played with are the Flower dress and the pale green Floating Circles and the grey waistcoat (both on page 71). The waistcoat was one of my first garments. Like much of my work, it is totally improvised as I knit. I soon learned that if you repeat patterns across a row, it not only is easier to memorize than a random sequence but also gives the work the illusion of being well planned.

Breaking away from rows of repeating patterns into a flowing random design is not at all difficult, if you can muster the confidence to just pick up the needles and let the design flow. Put the work up conti-

nually and stand back from it to see how it is progressing. Be careful not to line up motifs in those rows or to put motifs directly above each other. The Chinese snuff bottles (page 71) would make a gorgeous source to work from.

PERSIAN POPPY WAISTCOAT

The luxurious silk yarn in Chinese porcelain colours gives the colour scheme for this waistcoat a unique quality in a long line of my Persian Poppy variations. I 'courted' the V&A's Chinese figures, with their lotus offerings and harmonious garments, before starting work on this colour story. I have always loved the glowing pastel palette characteristic of some Chinese porcelain, and the V&A has a superb collection of this range. Chinese enamels are also a particularly good inspiration, if you like fine detail and clear, delicate colours.

YARNS FOR PERSIAN POPPY WAISTCOAT

Average yarn weight used – lightweight double knitting (sport)
Rowan *Lightweight DK* in the foll 5 colours:

    A (#76) willow – 25[50:50]g (1[1¾: 1¾]oz)

    B (#20) peach – 25g (1oz)

    C (#123) sea – 25g (1oz)

    D (#41) lipstick – 25g (1oz)

    E (#95) mulberry – 25g (1oz)

Rowan *Botany* in the foll colour:

    F (#34) lime – 50[75:100]g (1¾[2¾: 3½]oz)

Rowan *Mulberry Silk* in the foll 9 colours:

    G (#871) sorbet – 50g (1¾oz)

    H (#877) peony – 50[50:100]g (1¾ [1¾:3½]oz)

    I (#880) nightshade – 50g (1¾oz)

    J (#883) peppermint – 50[50:100]g (1¾[1¾:3½]oz)

Pages 72 and 73: The colours of these Chinese figures translated deliciously into the silks and cottons of my Persian Poppy shawl and waistcoat.

Opposite page: The Chinese porcelain colours of the Persian Poppy waistcoat, glowing in the moist air of Hampstead Heath.

Left: Persian Poppy waistcoat and shawl.

L (#872) flamingo – 50g (1¾oz)
M (#882) Aegean – 50g (1¾oz)
N (#879) orchid – 50g (1¾oz)
O (#878) fondant – 50g (1¾oz)
Q (#873) blush – 50g (1¾oz)
Rowan *Fine Cotton Chenille* in the foll 2 colours:
R (#383) turquoise – 50g (1¾oz)
S (#387) Saville – 50g (1¾oz)
Rowan *Cabled Mercerised Cotton* in the foll 2 colours:
T (#307) metallic – 50g (1¾oz)
U (#303) grass – 50g (1¾oz)
Rowan *Salad Days* in the foll colour:
V (#568) bright pink – 50g (1¾oz)
Rowan *Sea Breeze* in the foll 2 colours:
W (#539) Bermuda – 50[50:100]g (1¾
[1¾:3½]oz)
Y (#534) frolic – 50g (1¾oz)

NEEDLES
One pair each of 3¼mm (US size 3) and 4mm (US size 6) needles and circular needle 80cm (29″) long in each size *or size to obtain correct tension (gauge)*

SIZES AND MEASUREMENTS
To fit 86[91:96]cm (34[36:38]″) bust
Actual width across back 48[51:53]cm (19¼[20:21¼]″)
Length to shoulder 53[54:55]cm (21 [21¼:21¾]″)
Figures for larger sizes are given in square brackets; where there is only one set of figures, it applies to all sizes.

TENSION (GAUGE)
25½ sts and 27 rows to 10cm (4″) over colour patt on 4mm (US size 6) needles

Check your tension (gauge) before beginning.

NOTES
When using two colours in a row, carry colour not in use loosely across back of work, weaving it around working yarn.
Read charts from right to left for RS (knit) rows and from left to right for WS (purl) rows. Use 1 strand of yarn where there is only one letter to represent the colour, and 2 strands of yarn where there are 2 letters, i.e. 'UF' means one strand each of U and F.

BACK
Using 3¼mm (US size 3) needles and A, cast on 123[129:135] sts.
*Beg with a P row, work 9 rows in st st to form hem, so ending with a WS row.
Change to 4mm (US size 6) needles and beg colour patt as foll:
1st row (RS) Using A, purl (to form hemline).
2nd row Using G, purl.*
Beg with a K row, cont in st st foll chart 1 from 3rd chart row, rep first-26th rows for poppy patt and foll colour sequence table for colours, until back measures 31cm (12¼″) from hemline, ending with a WS row.

ARMHOLE SHAPING
Keeping patt correct, cast (bind) off 5[6:7] sts at beg of next 2 rows.
Dec 1 st at each end of next row and then dec 1 st at each end of every alternate row 8[9:10] times more.
95[97:99] sts.
Cont in patt without shaping until armhole measures 22[23:24]cm (8¾[9: 9½]″), ending with a WS row.

□ = background colour
☒ = poppy colour

NOTE See colour sequence table for actual colours.

CHART 1

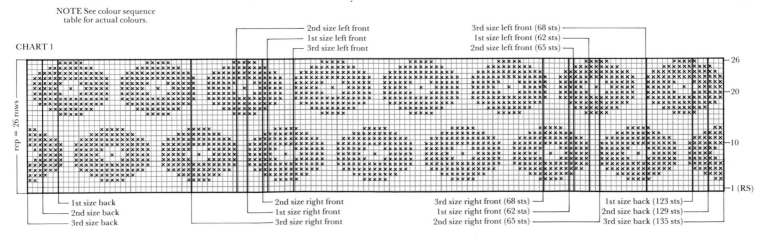

COLOUR SEQUENCE

row(s)	☒	☐	row(s)	☒	☐	row(s)	☒	☐
1	—	A	55-56	D	M	106	—	J
2	—	G	57	S	M	107-109	D	J
3-5	H	G	58	S	R	110-111	N	J
6	H	FF	59-60	N	R	112	Q	J
7-10	I	FF	61	O	R	113-116	Q	M
11-13	H	J	62-64	O	T	117	O	I
14-15	—	J	65	G	T	118	—	I
16-18	H	J	66	—	T	119	—	T
19-20	H	A	67	—	C	120	O	T
21-23	L	A	68-69	E	C	121	O	M
24-26	L	M	70	E	WW	122	O	WW
27	—	M	71	V	WW	123	Q	WW
28	—	R	72-75	V	UF	124	Q	G
29-30	L	R	76-78	V	M	125-126	YY	G
31	N	R	79	—	M	127	E	G
32-34	N	J	80	—	WW	128-130	E	J
35-37	B	J	81-82	YY	WW	131-132	—	J
38	B	M	83	YY	J	133-134	V	FF
39	O	M	84	L	J	135	S	FF
40	—	M	85-86	S	J	136-139	S	WW
41	—	C	87-88	H	J	140	N	M
42	O	C	89-91	H	UF	141-143	Q	M
43	O	T	92	—	UF			
44-45	Q	T	93	—	M			
46	N	T	94-96	L	M			
47-48	L	T	97-98	N	T			
49-50	L	I	99-100	Q	T			
51-52	N	I	101	O	T			
53	—	I	102-104	O	WW			
54	—	M	105	—	WW			

Rep from first row.

NOTE Where there are 2 letters, 2 strands of yarn are used, i.e. 'FF' means 2 strands of F.

SHOULDER AND NECK SHAPING

Keeping patt correct throughout, cast (bind) off 7 sts at the beg of next 2 rows.

81[83:85] sts. Divide for neck on next row as foll:

Next row (RS) Cast (bind) off 7 sts, patt 24 sts including st already on needle, cast (bind) off 19[21:23] centre sts, patt to end.

Next row (WS) Cast (bind) off 7 sts, patt to neck edge, slip rem sts (right shoulder) onto a spare needle (see foll Note). 24 sts at each side of neck.

Note If desired, work both sides of neck at same time with separate balls of yarn.

Left: I am particularly pleased with the sharp lime that borders the waistcoat.

CHART 2

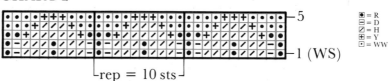

● = R
⊟ = D
⊘ = H
⊞ = Y
⊡ = WW

— 5

— 1 (WS)

└rep = 10 sts┘

Right: Being knitted in finer yarns than I usually use makes the Persian Poppy shawl drape gracefully.

LEFT NECK AND SHOULDER EDGES

Cast (bind) off 4 sts at beg of next row (neck edge), 8 sts at beg of next row (shoulder edge) and 4 sts at beg of next row. Cast (bind) off rem 8 sts.

RIGHT NECK AND SHOULDER EDGES

With WS facing, rejoin yarn to neck edge of sts at other side of neck and cast (bind) off 4 sts, patt to end. Complete as for left neck and shoulder edges.

FRONTS

<u>Note</u> *If desired, work both fronts at same time with separate balls of yarn.*

Using 3¼mm (US size 3) needles and A, cast on 62[65:68] sts. Work as for back from * to *.

Beg with a K row, cont in st st foll chart 1 from 3rd chart row (between chart markers for left or right front), rep first-26th rows for poppy patt and foll colour sequence table for colours, until there are 7[11:13] rows less than back to armhole, ending at front edge.

NECK SHAPING

Keeping patt correct throughout, dec 1 st at neck edge on next row and then every 4th row, AND AT THE SAME TIME when there are same number of rows as back to armhole, cast (bind) off 5[6:7] sts at armhole edge on next row, dec 1 st at armhole edge on next row and then on every alternate row 8[9:10] times more.

Cont dec 1 st at neck edge every 4th row until 35[36:37] sts rem, then dec 1 st at neck edge every 3rd row until 30 sts rem. Work without shaping until there are same number of rows as back to shoulder, ending at armhole edge.

SHOULDER SHAPING

Cast (bind) off 7 sts at beg of next row, then cast (bind) off on every alternate row at shoulder edge 7 sts once, 8 sts once. Work 1 row without shaping. Cast (bind) off rem 8 sts.

ARMBANDS

Press all pieces lightly on WS with a warm iron over a dry cloth. Using backstitch, join shoulder seams.

Using 3¼mm (US size 3) needles and A and with RS facing, pick up and K116

[120:124] sts evenly around armhole. Purl 1 row H, knit 1 row Y. Purl 2 rows F to form hemline. Beg with a P row, work 3 rows more in st st.

Cast (bind) off loosely.

FRONT BAND

Using backstitch, join side and armband seams. Fold hem at lower edge to WS along hemline and slipstitch in place.

Using 4mm (US size 6) circular needle and A and with RS facing, beg at lower right front edge and pick up and K74 [70:68] sts evenly up right front to beg of neck shaping, 59[67:73] sts along shaped front edge, 45[47:49] sts across back neck, 59[67:73] sts along shaped left front edge and 74[70:68] sts from beg of neck shaping to lower left front edge. 311[321:331] sts.

Beg with a P row and working back and forth in rows in st st, work colour patt foll chart 2 from first chart row until all 5 chart rows have been worked, so ending with a WS row.

Change to 3¼mm (US size 3) circular needle and using 2 strands of F, knit 2 rows to form hemline. Using one strand of F and beg with a K row, work 12 rows in st st. Cast (bind) off loosely.

FINISHING

Fold front band and armbands to WS along hemline and slipstitch in place. Press seams lightly on WS with a warm iron over a dry cloth.

PERSIAN POPPY SHAWL

My shawls are designed to involve you in playing with colours. The shawl is begun with three stitches for the centre point and then shaped by increasing one stitch at each end of every following row. The first third of the shawl goes so fast that you are hooked before it starts to get a bit more laborious to work across the longer rows.

I just knit up the shawl until it measures about 2 metres (6 feet) across the top of the triangle or until it is a good length in back when draped around the shoulders. The top of the shawl has a hem added in an attractive colour or stripe, and it is then fringed in either one or many colours. When choosing colours for the shawl, if you use those specified in the Persian Poppy waistcoat and add about ten similar shades, you will come pretty close to the colouring shown.

YARNS FOR PERSIAN POPPY SHAWL

Average yarn weight used – lightweight double knitting (sport)
Approx 350g (12½oz) in a mixture of yarns and colours for background A
Approx 600g (21oz) in a mixture of yarns and colours for poppies B

NEEDLES

One pair of 4mm (US size 6) needles *or size to obtain correct tension*
One 3¼mm (US size 3) and one 4mm (US size 6) circular needle 100cm (39″) long

MEASUREMENTS

181cm (72½″) across top by 91cm (36½″) deep, excluding fringe

TENSION (GAUGE)

27 sts and 27 rows to 10cm (4″) over colour patt on 4mm (US size 6) needles
Check your tension (gauge) before beginning.

NOTES

When using two colours in a row, carry colour not in use loosely across back of work, weaving it around working yarn.
Read chart from right to left for RS (knit) rows and from left to right for WS (purl) rows.

TO MAKE

Using 4mm (US size 6) needles and A, cast on 3 sts.
Knit 1 row.
Working in random stripes of A (background colours) as desired, cont in st st inc 1 st at each end of next 7 rows, so ending with a WS row.

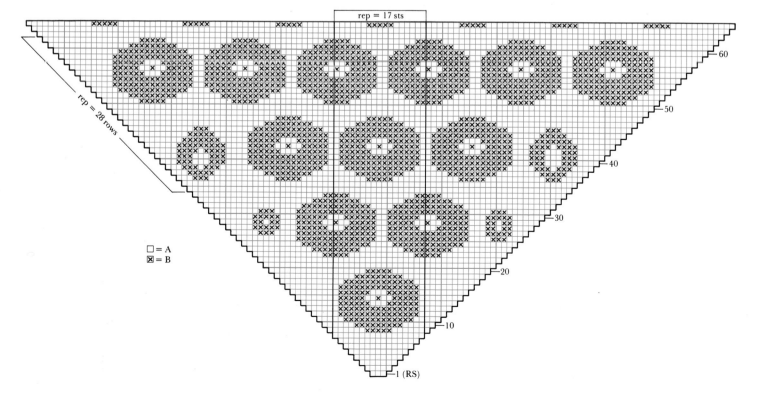

□ = A
☒ = B

*Right: Some of the
infinite variations of
the Persian Poppy
design, with a
modern glass vase on
shirt fabric to suggest
a new shape for this
theme.*

Cont in st st inc 1 st at each end of every row and foll chart from 9th chart row for poppy patt, changing colours for random stripes on different rows for B (poppies) and A (background), until 65th chart row has been completed.

Cont in poppy patt as set inc 1 st at each end of every row, changing to 4mm (US size 6) circular needle when there are too many sts to fit comfortably on straight needles, and adding to number of poppies in each band of poppies until 17 bands of poppies have been worked from beg, so ending with a WS row. 244 rows and 489 sts.

Change to 3¼mm (US size 3) circular needle and using A, knit 2 rows without shaping to form hemline.

Beg with a K row, work in st st for 12 rows, working in random stripes of A and dec 1 st at each end of every row.

Cast (bind) off.

FINISHING

Fold hem at top of shawl to WS along hemline and slipstitch in place. Press lightly on WS with a warm iron over a dry cloth.

FRINGE

For each fringe cut eight 46cm (18″) long strands of 1 shade of B. Fold strands in half to form a loop. With WS of shawl facing, insert a crochet hook from front to back through edge of shawl at one corner and draw loop through. Then draw the ends through the loop and pull tightly to secure the fringe knot. Knot fringe in the same way along both diagonal sides of the shawl working one knot at the lower tip and 114 evenly spaced along each side, using random shades of B, changing every two fringes.

JAPANESE LICHEN SHAWL

The shapes for the Japanese Lichen shawl grew out of my love of lichens, one of the outstanding features of the British countryside.

I designed it for an exhibition in Japan, wanting to express my love of the subtleties of Japanese taste. Their endless fascination with dark, restrained tones led me to choose a very close range of gunmetal greys, silvers and hints of grey-pinks. I was lucky to find a wonderful selection of textures – silks, bouclés, softly shaded ribbons and mohair, wool-rayon mixtures and some glorious dark tweeds, all in my chosen colour range.

Only a section of the shawl is given here, to show you the simple theory behind the random design. The outline and background colours are carried across the back, while the differing lichen centres are worked in place. I never put anything on paper myself, but preferably improvise as I go. This gives you the delicious sense of risk and fascination to see how it is all going to turn out. As riveting as a good mystery story!

YARNS FOR JAPANESE LICHEN SHAWL

Average yarn weight used – Aran (heavy worsted)

Approx 500g (17½oz) in a mixture of yarns and colours in dark shades for background A

Approx 350g (12½oz) in a mixture of yarns and colours in medium shades for lichen B

Approx 200g (7oz) in a mixture of yarns and colours in light shades for lichen outlines C

NEEDLES

One pair of 5mm (US size 8) needles *or size to obtain correct tension*

One 3¾mm (US size 5) and one 5mm (US size 8) circular needle 100cm (39″) long

MEASUREMENTS

162cm (65″) across top by 81cm (32½″) deep, excluding fringe

TENSION (GAUGE)

21 sts and 21 rows to 10cm (4″) over colour patt on 5mm (US size 8) needles
Check your tension (gauge) before beginning.

NOTES

Only a section of the shawl has been charted to give an idea of the lichen shapes. The shapes can

*Opposite page:
Japanese Lichen
shawl, with a dark
version of my
Tumbling Boxes
crewneck done in silk
and wool.*

*Below right: A
detail of the Japanese
Lichen shawl,
showing the many
shades and textures of
yarn used within a
quite restricted colour
range.*

be worked freehand as the shawl is knitted from the tip upwards or it can be charted on a large piece of graph paper. To chart the entire shawl, first draw the shawl outline onto the graph paper. The shawl is begun with 3 sts (see poppy shawl chart on page 79) and 1 stitch is increased at each end of every row over 170 rows until there are 341 stitches across the top. Draw lichen shapes freely onto the graph paper using the charted section as a rough guide.

Read chart from right to left for RS (knit) rows and from left to right for WS (purl) rows.

Work background in random stripes of A and carry A, when not in use, loosely across back of work weaving it around working yarn on every 3rd or 4th st. Work each lichen shape in random stripes of B and lichen outlines in C. Do not carry B and C across back, but use a separate length of each of B and C for each area of colour, twisting yarns when changing colours to avoid holes.

TO MAKE

Using 5mm (US size 8) needles and A, cast on 3 sts.

Knit 1 row.

Working in random stripes of A (back-ground colours) as desired, cont in st st inc 1 st at each end of next 5 rows, so ending with a WS row.

Cont in st st, working in lichen colour patt (see <u>Note</u> above for charting the lichen shapes) and inc 1 st at each end of every row, changing to 5mm (US size 8) circular needle when there are too many sts to fit comfortably on straight needles, until there are 341 sts (170 rows), so ending with a WS row.

Change to 3¾mm (US size 5) circular needle and using A, knit 2 rows without shaping to form hemline.

Beg with a K row, work in st st for 12 rows working in random stripes of A and dec 1 st at each end of every row.

Cast (bind) off.

FINISHING

Fold hem at top of shawl to WS along hemline and slipstitch in place. Press lightly on WS with a warm iron.

FRINGE

For each fringe cut six 56cm (22″) long strands of mixed colours of A. Fold strands in half to form a loop. With WS of shawl facing, insert a crochet hook from front to back through edge of shawl at one corner and draw loop through. Then draw the ends through the loop and pull tightly to secure the fringe knot. Knot fringe in the same way along both diagonal sides of the shawl, working one knot at the lower tip and 63 evenly spaced along each side.

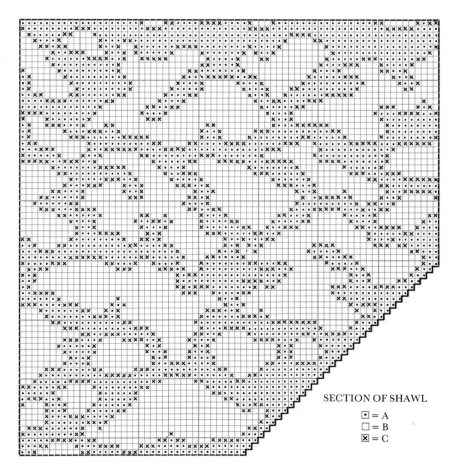

SECTION OF SHAWL

⊡ = A
□ = B
☒ = C

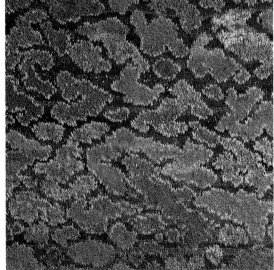

SQUARES AND PATCHES

Why is the simple square so eternally satisfying as a design element? The baby's first building blocks and the patchwork on the cot start the mind playing with this warm, balanced form. Later, this early acquaintance is continued through playing board games like chess and working on graph paper.

My first attempt at patterns in knitting were chequerboards, and after twenty years I still love doing variations on squares when designing on the needles. It's easy to improvise square forms in knitting without resorting to a design on graph paper.

Looking for variations on the square in different cultures' design is enthralling. Japan employs the most dramatic use of squares in the Kabuki and Nö drama. Old Japanese woodcuts are filled with strong square plaids and many other inventive uses of squares, from the boldest to the finest in scale. African fabrics and wall decorations are another rich source of squares.

In my early twenties, when I travelled east through Turkey, Syria and Afghanistan, I found the rich array of overlapping carpets on mosque and coffee house floors an interesting variation on this design theme. My first colour stimulus for squares in the Near East came from viewing the heavily patched clothes of the Islamic peasants and the patched

Right: The Squares shawl covered with a collection of stamps in lovely faded colours.

sails on their fishing boats. Faded grey-blues and shades of rich brown spiced with a shot of lavender or dull pink – delicious and timeless!

BLUE PATCH CREWNECK

Deep blues and greens always give me a lift, and the Islamic pots in turquoise, royal blue and clear grass green at the V&A thrill me to the core. Every time I see them I find them more satisfying.

The Chinese collection at the V&A also has outstanding examples of pure turquoise, as well as other colours, in graceful shapes. All this was a high point indeed from which to start my Blue Patch sweater. I feel that the large plain areas of the patches echo the simple masses of the pots.

YARNS FOR BLUE PATCH CREWNECK

Average yarn weight used – Aran (heavy worsted)
Rowan *Lightweight DK* in the foll 9 colours:

- A (#501) hyacinth – 50[75]g (1¾ [2¾]oz)
- B (#56) royal blue – 75g (2¾oz)
- C (#125) turquoise – 100g (3½oz)
- D (#100) deep jade – 25[50]g (1 [1¾]oz)
- E (#89) pale jade – 25g (1oz)
- F (#55) medium blue – 50[75]g (1¾ [2¾]oz)
- G (#417) deep ocean – 25g (1oz)
- H (#90) bright jade – 200[250]g (7 [9]oz)
- I (#51) deep sky – 25[50]g (1[1¾]oz)

Rowan *Wool Twist* in the foll 2 colours:
- J (#155) charcoal – 100g (3½oz)
- L (#152) blue – 100g (3½oz)

Rowan *Fleck DK* in the foll 2 colours:
- M (#56F) royal blue – 50[100]g (1¾ [3½]oz)
- N (#51F) deep sky – 100g (3½oz)

Rowan *Light Tweed* in the foll 4 colours:
- O (#221) Pacific – 100[125]g (3½ [4½]oz)
- Q (#222) lakeland – 25g (1oz)
- R (#220) jade – 25g (1oz)
- S (#213) lavender – 25g (1oz)

Rowan *Rowanspun Tweed* in the foll 2 colours:
- T (#757) iris – 100g (3½oz)
- U (#758) confetti – 100g (3½oz)

Rowan *Fine Fleck Tweed* in the foll colour:
- V (#51) deep sky – 75[100]g (2¾ [3½]oz)

NEEDLES

One pair each of 3¾mm (US size 5) and 4½mm (US size 7) needles *or size to obtain correct tension (gauge)*

SIZES AND MEASUREMENTS

To fit 86-96[102-112]cm (34-38[40-44]″) bust or chest
Actual width across back 54[60]cm (21¾[24]″)
Length to shoulder 61[65]cm (24¼[26]″)
Sleeve length 48cm (19¼″)
Figures for larger sizes are given in square brackets; where there is only one set of figures, it applies to both sizes.

TENSION (GAUGE)

18 sts and 25 rows to 10cm (4″) over colour patt on 4½mm (US size 7) needles
Check your tension (gauge) before beginning.

NOTES

When working colour patt, do not carry yarn across back of work, but use a separate length of each colour for each area of colour, twisting yarns when changing colours to avoid holes.
Read chart from right to left for RS (knit) rows and from left to right for WS (purl) rows.
Use 1 strand of yarn where there is only one letter and 2 strands where there are two letters, i.e. 'CO' means 1 strand each of C and O.

BACK

*Using 3¾mm (US size 5) needles and AA, cast on 83[91] sts.
Change to J and beg K1, P1 rib as foll:
1st rib row (RS) K1, (P1, K1) to end.
2nd rib row P1, (K1, P1) to end.
Rep last 2 rows until 19 rib rows have been completed, ending with a RS row.
Next row (inc row) Rib 7[6], make 1 st by picking up horizontal loop lying before next st and working into the back of it – called make 1 –, (rib 5, make 1) 14[16]

times, rib 6[5]. 98[108] sts.
Change to 4½mm (US size 7) needles and beg with a K row, work 4[10] rows in st st, so ending with a WS row.
Beg with a K row, cont in st st foll chart from 11th chart row, until 78th[82nd] chart row has been completed.
Mark last row for position of armholes.*
Cont in colour patt foll chart until 144th[148th] chart row has been completed, so ending with a WS row.

SHOULDER AND NECK SHAPING
Divide for neck on next row as foll:
145th[149th] chart row (RS) Cast (bind) off 10[12] sts, patt 26[28] sts including st already on needle, cast (bind) off 26[28] centre sts, patt to end.
146th[150th] chart row Cast (bind) off 10[12] sts, patt to neck edge, slip rem sts (right shoulder) onto a spare needle (see foll Note). 26[28] sts at each side of neck.
Note If desired, work both sides of neck at same time with separate balls of yarn.

LEFT NECK AND SHOULDER EDGES
Keeping patt correct throughout, cast (bind) off 3 sts at beg of next row (neck edge).
Cast (bind) off 11[12] sts at beg of next row (shoulder edge) and dec 1 st at end (neck edge). Work 1 row without shaping. Cast (bind) off rem 11[12] sts.

RIGHT NECK AND SHOULDER EDGES
With WS facing, rejoin yarn to neck edge of sts at other side of neck and cast (bind) off 3 sts, patt to end. Work as for left neck and shoulder edges from ** to **.

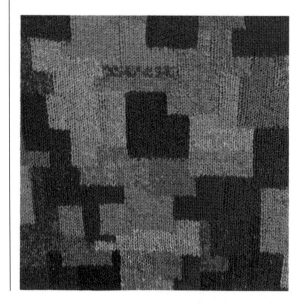

Right: This patch format is an excellent pattern structure for any colour scheme you fancy. The muted tones of old Italian frescoes would be handsome.

FRONT
Work as for back from * to *. Cont in colour patt foll chart until 120th[124th] chart row has been completed, so ending with a WS row.

NECK SHAPING
Divide for neck on next row as foll:
121st[125th] chart row (RS) Patt 44[48] sts, cast (bind) off 10[12] centre sts, patt to end.
122nd[126th] chart row Patt to neck edge, slip rem sts (left shoulder) on to a spare needle (see foll Note). 44[48] sts at each side of neck.
Note If desired, work both sides of neck at same time with separate balls of yarn.

RIGHT NECK AND SHOULDER EDGES
Keeping patt correct throughout, cast (bind) off 3 sts at beg of next row (neck edge), cast (bind) off at neck edge on every alternate row 2 sts twice, then dec 1 st at neck edge on every alternate row 5 times. 32[36] sts.
Work without shaping until 145th[149th] chart row has been completed, so ending with a RS row.
***Beg shoulder shaping as foll:
Cast (bind) off 10[12] sts at beg of next row and 11[12] sts at beg of foll alternate row. Work 1 row without shaping.
Cast (bind) off rem 11[12] sts.***

LEFT NECK AND SHOULDER EDGES
With WS facing, rejoin yarn at neck edge to sts at other side of neck and cast (bind) off 3 sts, patt to end.
Cast (bind) off at neck edge on every alternate row 2 sts twice, then dec 1 st at neck edge on every alternate row 5 times. 32[36] sts. Work without shaping until 144th[148th] chart row has been completed, so ending with a WS row.
Complete as for right neck and shoulder edges from *** to ***.

SLEEVES
Note If desired, work both sleeves at same time with separate balls of yarn.
Using 3¾mm (US size 5) needles and AA, cast on 43 sts.
Using J, work in K1, P1 rib patt as for back until 19 rib rows have been completed, so ending with a RS row.

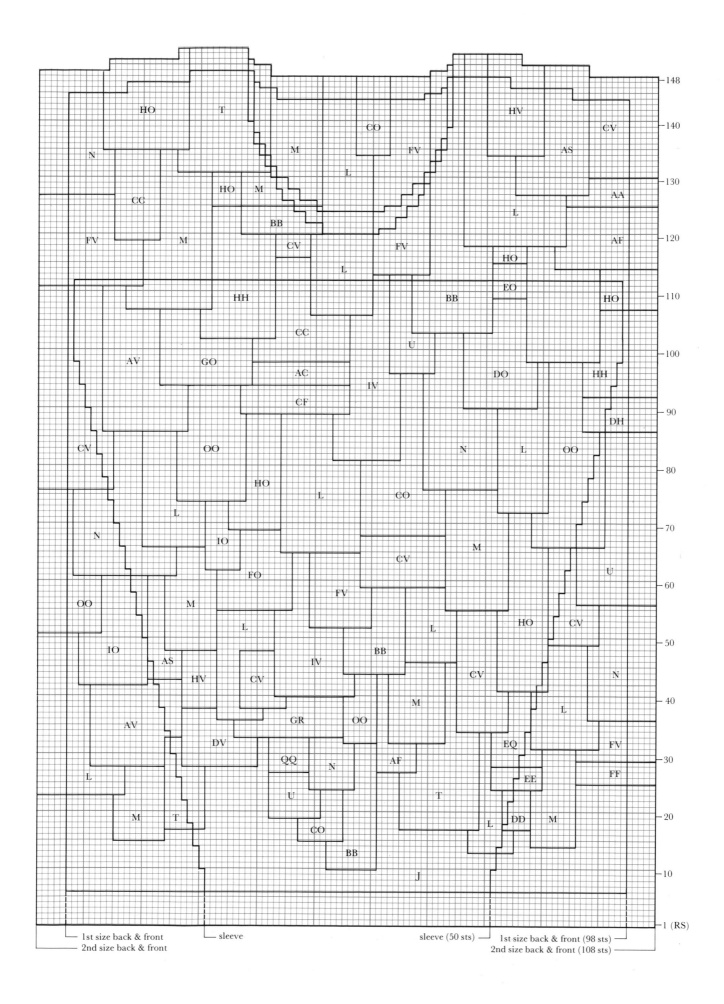

*This page and
opposite page: This
multi-disciplined
collection of decorated
objects from the
V&A shows how
versatile a simple
square can be. (See
page 156 for
descriptions of objects
shown here.)*

Next row (inc row) Rib 4, make 1, (rib 6,
make 1) 6 times, rib 3. 50 sts.
Change to 4½mm (US size 7) needles
and beg with a K row, work 4 rows in st
st, so ending with a WS row.
Beg with a K row, cont in st st foll chart
from 11th chart row, AND AT THE SAME
TIME shape sleeve by inc 1 st at each end
of next row and then every 4th row until
there are 96 sts.
Work in patt without shaping until 112th
chart row has been completed or until
sleeve is required length.
Cast (bind) off loosely.

NECKBAND

Press all pieces lightly on WS with a
warm iron over a damp cloth, omitting
ribbing. Join right shoulder seam.
Using 3¾mm (US size 5) needles and BB
and with RS facing, pick up and K
66[68] sts evenly along front neck and
39[41] sts across back neck. 105[109] sts.
Beg K1, P1 rib as foll:
1st rib row (WS) Using BB, P1, (K1, P1)
to end.
2nd rib row Using T, K1, (P1, K1) to end.
First and 2nd rib rows form rib patt.
Work 6 rows more in rib patt in stripes as
foll:
1 row CC, 4 rows BB, 1 row T.
Using AA, cast (bind) off loosely in rib.

FINISHING

Join left shoulder and neckband seam.
Join cast (bound) off edge of sleeves to
back and front between markers, matching centre of top of sleeve to shoulder
seam. Join side and sleeve seams.
Press seams lightly on WS with a warm
iron over a damp cloth, omitting ribbing.

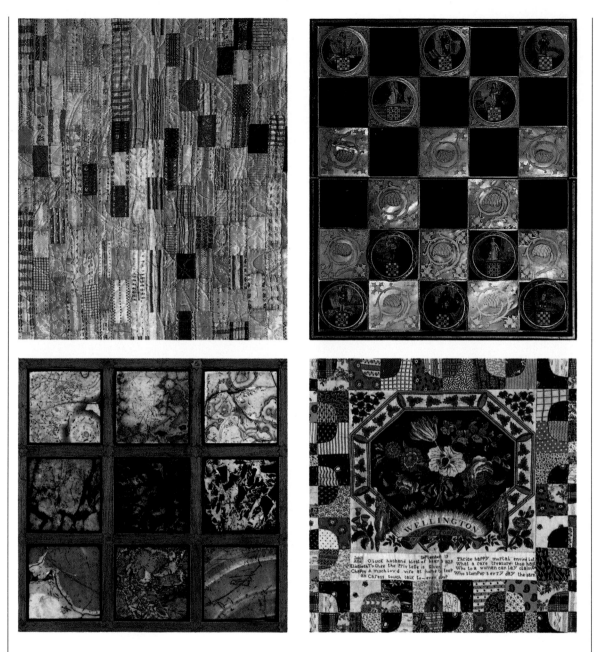

Overleaf: The Window V-neck, which was the inspiration for the Windows coat kit. Notice how the forty colours of the coat are used in different combinations to expand the colour range.

WINDOW V-NECK

This blocky design started life on one of the many plane journeys I have made since *Glorious Knitting* was published. I used to be a very easily bored, restless traveller, with my long legs making lengthy flights a strain. When I started taking projects like knitting or needle-point on these trips, I found the time whizzed by, and journeys became measured in terms of 'that poppy scarf' or 'the back of the Roman waistcoat'. One of these trips found me with a delicious muted range of colours in fine textures; and by the time we touched down in New York I was casting off a small oblong swatch, which later attracted admiration

from friends and colleagues in that city. One of the admirers commissioned me to do a V-neck sweater based on it. When that was completed it caught the eye of Stephen Sheard at Rowan Yarns, who commissioned the Windows coat. This became my most ambitious kit to date. I put forty colours of differing yarns and textures into the coat kit, and it does seem to appeal to a wide range of souls, young and old.

With this V-neck pattern you can work all the areas of colour in intarsia, or you can carry the outline colour across the back of the other colours. The secret of these colours is to keep them medium in value, or a little darker if need be, but

to avoid any light tones. Any dusky tweed colours will do with a few richer tones to lift the effect. Of course, you could use this chart to do any colour scheme you feel like, or have yarns for. For a completely different look the whole thing could be done in very dark tones or really pale ones.

YARNS FOR WINDOW V-NECK

Average yarn weight used – double knitting (worsted)

A total of approx 750g (27oz) in a mixture of yarns and colours

NEEDLES

One pair each of 3¾mm (US size 5) and 4½mm (US size 7) needles *or size to obtain correct tension (gauge)*

One 3¾mm (US size 5) circular needle 40cm (15½") long

SIZE AND MEASUREMENTS

One size to fit up to 107cm (42") bust or chest

Actual width across back 58cm (23")
Length to shoulder 61cm (24¼")
Sleeve length 48cm (19¼")

TENSION (GAUGE)

19 sts and 26 rows to 10cm (4") over colour patt on 4½mm (US size 7) needles
Check your tension (gauge) before beginning.

NOTES

When working plaid border, carry colour not in use (except for single-stitch vertical stripes) loosely across back of work, weaving it around working yarn. Work single-stitch vertical stripes with a separate length of yarn.

When working colour patt above plaid border, do not carry yarn across back of work, but use a separate length of each colour for each area of colour, twisting yarns when changing colours to avoid holes.

Read chart from right to left for RS (knit) rows and from left to right for WS (purl) rows.

BACK

*Using 3¾mm (US size 5) needles and desired colour, cast on 97 sts.
Changing colour for every row, beg K1,

P1 rib on next row as foll:
<u>1st rib row</u> (RS) K1, (P1, K1) to end.
<u>2nd rib row</u> P1, (K1, P1) to end.
Last 2 rows form rib patt.
Using a different colour for each row, work in rib patt for 3cm (1¼"), ending with a RS row.
<u>Next row</u> (inc row) Rib 6, make 1 st by picking up horizontal loop lying before next st and working into the back of it – called make 1 –, (rib 7, make 1) 12 times, rib 7. 110 sts.
Change to 4½mm (US size 7) needles and beg with a K row, work in st st foll chart from first chart row in 6 desired colours for plaid patt, until 22nd chart row has been completed.
Cont in st st foll chart from 23rd chart row, changing colours for large patches and central squares as desired and keeping patch outline colour the same throughout*, until 150th chart row has been completed, so ending with a WS row.

SHOULDER SHAPING

Keeping patt correct, cast (bind) off 13 sts at beg of next 2 rows and 12 sts at beg of next 4 rows.
Slip rem 36 sts onto spare needle for back neck to be used later for neckband.

FRONT

Work as for back from * to *, using same colours as for back, until 99th chart row has been completed, so ending with a RS row.

Overleaf: This Sion Gospel book cover in the V&A is an early example of squares used in decoration.

Page 97: Just some of the many possibilities that the simple square can produce as an inventive structure for colour – from rows of little boxes to interwoven ribbons and Byzantine jewel-studded squares.

Left: You can see that this design would lend itself to several quite different colour moods. This dusky tweed colour scheme contains neither very light nor very dark tones.

NECK SHAPING

Divide for neck on next row as foll:

Next row (WS) Patt 53 sts, work 2 sts tog, slip rem sts (left shoulder) onto a spare needle (see foll Note).

Note *If desired, work both sides of neck at same time with separate balls of yarn.*

RIGHT NECK AND SHOULDER EDGES

Keeping patt correct throughout, work 2 rows without shaping.

Dec 1 st at neck edge on next row and then on every 3rd row until 37 sts rem, so ending with a RS row (151st chart row).

Keeping neck edge straight, cast (bind) off 13 sts at beg of next row, then cast (bind) off 12 sts at beg of foll alternate row. Work 1 row without shaping.

Cast (bind) off rem 12 sts.

LEFT NECK AND SHOULDER EDGES

With WS facing, rejoin yarn at neck edge to sts at other side of neck and work 2 sts tog, patt to end. 54 sts. Keeping patt correct, work 2 rows without shaping.

Dec 1 st at neck edge on next row and then on every 3rd row until 38 sts rem, so ending with a WS row (150th chart row).

151st chart row (RS) Cast (bind) off 13 sts, patt to last 2 sts, work 2 sts tog.

Work 1 row without shaping.

Cast (bind) off 12 sts at beg of next row. Work 1 row without shaping. Cast (bind) off rem 12 sts.

SLEEVES

Note *If desired, work both sleeves at same time with separate balls of yarn.*

Using 3¾mm (US size 5) needles and same colour as back, cast on 45 sts.

Work in K1, P1 rib patt as for back for 6cm (2½"), ending with a RS row.

Next row (inc row) Rib 2, make 1, (rib 5, make 1) 8 times, rib 3. 54 sts.

Change to 4½mm (US size 7) needles and beg with a K row, work in st st foll chart from first chart row and using same colours as for back, AND AT THE SAME TIME shape sleeve by inc 1 st at each end of every 4th row until there are 106 sts.

Work without shaping until 109th chart row has been completed or until sleeve measures required length.

Cast (bind) off loosely.

NECKBAND

Press all pieces lightly on WS with a warm iron over a damp cloth, omitting ribbing.

Using backstitch, join shoulder seams.

Using 3¾mm (US size 5) circular needle and desired colour and with RS facing, beg at left shoulder seam and pick up and K57 sts evenly down left front neck, 58 sts evenly up right front neck, K36 sts of back neck from spare needle. 151 sts.

Using desired colours throughout, beg K1, P1 rib as foll:

1st round P1, (K1, P1) 27 times, sl 1-K1-psso (centre front reached), K2 tog, (P1, K1) to end of round.

2nd round Rib to centre 4 sts of front neck, sl 1-K1-psso, K2 tog, rib to end.

Rep last round 5 times more.

Cast (bind) off loosely in rib, working decreases at centre front as before.

FINISHING

Mark back and front 28cm (11") from shoulder seams.

Using backstitch, join cast (bound) off edge of sleeves to back and front between markers, matching centre of top of sleeve to shoulder seam.

Join side and sleeve seams, using backstitch for st st and invisible seam for rib. Press seams lightly on WS with a warm iron over a damp cloth, omitting ribbing.

UNLIKELY SOURCES

Stone and brick walls are a constant source of design ideas, particularly in Britain. Every area of these islands has a style and colouring of stone that can feed the imagination of a designer. Some of my patch and square improvisations were inspired by the beauty of the stone walls of Scotland and the Lake District of England.

Mediterranean cultures have an astoundingly inventive way with walls. Malta, in particular, is like a honeycomb of delightfully individual stone walls. Some of the walls have surprising patches of sky blue, pink or white wash on them – the result of reusing stones from a collapsed farmhouse.

Opposite page: Here we see stone walls from London, Lancashire and Scotland, with some of my knitted designs inspired by those rich and varied sources. Pictured are (from top, left to right) the Patch shawl; Brick Diamond and Brick V-necks; Stone Patch jacket and Tumbling Boxes crewneck; Cross Patch V-neck kit; Cross Patch and Shirt Stripe Patch V-necks and Squares shawl; and Cross Patch coat.

FANCIFUL FLORA

The magic of flowers in decoration is eternal – as we can see in the arts and crafts of nearly all cultures. The frail, ephemeral quality of a flower amazes me again and again, especially after studying the decorative portraits of them painted on furniture and porcelain, woven and embroidered on fabrics and carved in wood and stone. They appear so solid and sturdy, while lighting up the objects they adorn. This most joyously universal of themes seems to bring a musical lightness to whatever it graces.

I myself find flowers a constantly renewing theme. In knitting I usually treat them in a stylized, flat manner, whereas I use a more realistic and detailed approach in my needlepoint.

As I write this I glance up at my studio pinboard, with its usual random choice of cards and cuttings that have caught my eye and seemed worth saving over the past few months, and find a host of floral motifs: a rose on a scrap of linoleum found in a skip (dumpster), fat Victorian roses decorating a sewing accessories packet, embroidered flowers from Yugoslavia, stylized painted flowers on a Chinese burial paper, and rows of tulips from a Turkish embroidery, knitted as a swatch for a new jacket. There is a lattice of eighteenth-century flowers from a chair back and a delicate painting of Japanese flowers. All these different

Left: Opulent lushness is what I was aiming for in this tea cosy. These overblown blooms on china in the V&A served as a rich inspiration for needlepoint.

flower moods, styles and colourings are just a taste of the millions of possibilities to be found, collected and then revitalized by the knitter and needlepointer.

Another related and recurring theme in decorations is the fruits and vegetables born of flowers. As I get older I find these objects more and more subtly beautiful. There is a sense of health and sanity about a basket full of fresh vegetables and ripe fruit which makes them beautiful subjects. Dutch, Italian, Turkish and Oriental paintings of fruit and vegetables enthrall me.

Familiar fruits like apples, pears and plums feature repeatedly in my textile work. I have found good sources of these subjects on dishes, box labels, wrapping paper and reproductions of old still lifes.

Working from sources in the V&A is a gift to a textile designer. From old embroideries to the wonderfully painted china, there are plenty of examples of strong, simple shapes of fruits and vegetables in interesting colours. Often I just

take the shape and add my own colour.

Look to the marketplaces around the world, as I have, to stimulate your designer's eye. Orderly piles of fruits and vegetables are as satisfying to view as most sculptures, antiques or gardens, with the added bonus that you can eat the visual display!

Greengrocers' stalls would make a wonderful subject for a needlepoint carpet or couch covering. Noticing how different countries lay out their produce should give us lots of ideas for textile pattern and colour arrangements. I recall markets in Morocco where olives, dates and figs were laid out on marble slabs in a design that was breathtaking in its masterly arrangement of shapes and colours. Some years, exhibitors at London's Chelsea Flower Show have proudly displayed great pyramids of cauliflowers, leeks and spring onions which are a joy to behold.

Japanese grocery stores are far more beautiful than most museums. The fish,

*Overleaf:
Needlepoint Flower
tea cosy in progress.*

———

*Opposite page and
below: Seen here
with the plate that
inspired the design
for the Flower tea
cosy are other
delicious flower
sources from the
V&A's extensive
collection (see 156).*

———

This page: The golden amber tones of wood grain (above) were used for a version of the Flower Pyramid cushion (below).

in particular, are the most astounding revelation. Somehow these sea creatures become like parts of a giant kaleidoscope design – rows of squid tentacles looking for all the world like a wonderful Fair Isle knitting pattern. Japan's bio-engineered fruit is a little too much larger than life for my taste, but it certainly makes an opulent display.

FLOWER TEA COSY

Many of the mad confections of flowers in the V&A collection of china could have inspired the intense explosion on my Flower tea cosy. The main arrangement came from a plate (page 102), and bits were added collage-fashion from other sources in the museum. For instance, the orange poppy in the lower right-hand corner is from the melon plate (page 125).

When stitching a cluttered grouping like this, I try to find flowers that have distinct markings. Pansies, ranunculuses and striped tulips are ideal subjects for needlepoint. Whatever distortions I create, the stitched blob of coloured tent-stitch pattern still probably reads as a flower.

It fascinates me how changing a background affects the colours of the arrangement. Placing this bouquet on a stormy air force blue seems to bring a deep glow to the colours, so different from the way they appear on the original white plate. Neutral grounds often enhance subtle colours. On the other hand, vivid colours like red, royal blue or yellow can give a great lift to a design. I try to be careful not to kill my subtle or soft colours with too hard a background, but sometimes am delightfully surprised how exciting a strong colour is. If you want a punchy colour but feel that it may overshadow the arrangement, choose a shade for your background that is just slightly greyed.

The borders on much of my work come from seeing the delightful and inventive patterned borders on china and decorative textiles of the past. Steve suggested the yellow and red border to echo the striped tulip. Broken colour, as in this border of little blocks, can usually benefit from strong, contrasting tones.

FLOWER NEEDLEPOINTS

There are many fantasy flowers at the V&A that can be used as sources for needlepoint. Early textiles and painted furniture include many examples of imaginary conglomerations of flower parts used to make bold decorative statements.

*Previous page (from
top left to right):
Flower Pyramid
cushion; Medallion
cushion; Bargello
Flower bench;
Bouquet cushion;
Delft table mats;
and Flower shoulder
bag – some of my
needlepoint
interpretations of the
inexhaustible flower
theme, all (except for
the bench cover and
Bouquet cushion)
available as kits (see
page 158).*

In my Bargello Flower bench (page 107), I was working from a mixture of English chintz flowers and some magnificent examples of fantasy blooms from a Persian carpet in the V&A. Carpet flowers are really rewarding to work from if you find shading a daunting task. They are usually rendered in a flat, easy-to-copy style, which makes them also ideal subjects for knitting. Rarely do they have enough colour when isolated from the whole design of the carpet, so do add that special richness that comes from an abundance of colour.

TURKISH CARNATION JACKET

Turkish Carnation is a double 'first' – it is the first design I interpreted directly from a textile at the V&A and the first knitting design I had published that was actually seen in the streets by its author. (In the early Sixties I had been commissioned by Judy Brittain of *Vogue Knitting* to do a waistcoat – my first professional design – but there was relatively little take-up on that. In those days few people were attempting knits with lots of colour changes.) You can imagine what a thrill it is to see a pattern you have struggled with, and tried to visualize 'in action', actually being worn. The Turkish Carnation was published in *Creative Dressing* (Routledge and Kegan Paul, 1980), a book by Kaori O'Connor which was ahead of its time. I have reworked the colouring and given it a more wearable collar, but have retained the same bold motifs which suit my sense of drama. Seeing it move down the street on a proud knitter's back is indeed a great excitement.

Do try other colour schemes. The original was cream on dusty pinks, but any fairly contrasting colouring would do. I could see it in a Russian-ballet mood with dark magenta flowers on brilliant buttercup gold, with high turquoise streaks in the blooms and royal blue bases to them.

The Carnation design could also be adapted for a most dramatic big coat, using the shape of the Jug coat (page

Right: The colours of this North London house and hedge complement this particular colouring of the Turkish Carnation jacket.

144). The flowers could be made a little larger, or more space could be left between them if the same number of stitches is to be used – 127 stitches for the jacket and 150 stitches for the coat. Of course a narrower coat could be made the same width as the jacket.

Whatever you end up doing, one thing I find important when working on a new colour scheme is to add the ribbing only after knitting the body of the garment. That way you can make the perfect 'frame' for your colour scheme. The ribbing can emphasize or diminish certain colours in the body, and so can either make or spoil an arrangement. Sometimes a light, bright edge lifts the colours, but often a deeper ribbing is called for. I

continued on p. 112

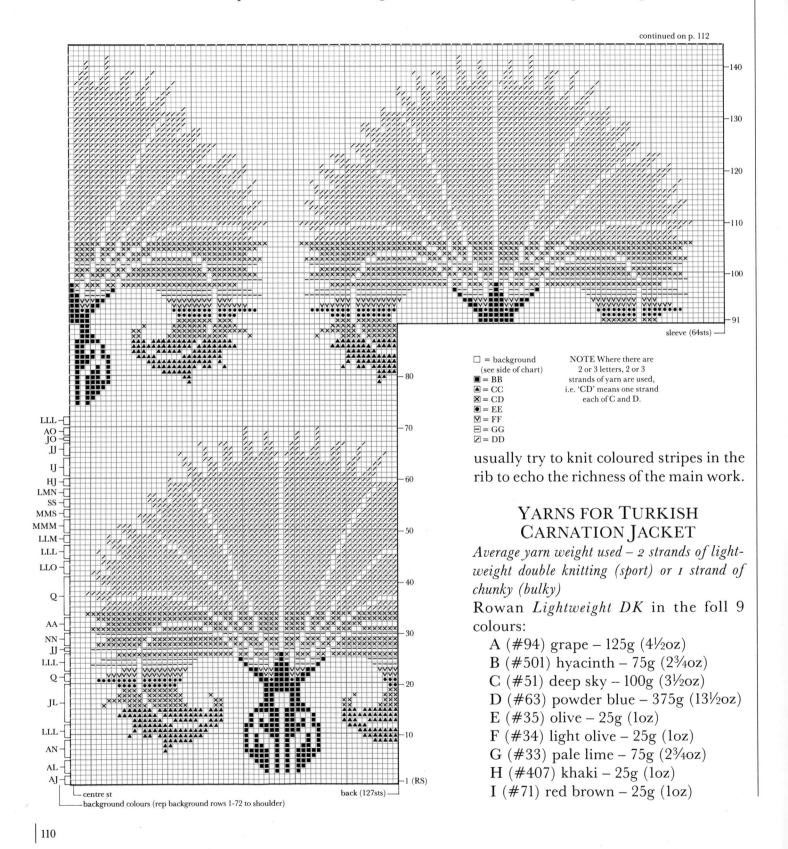

□ = background (see side of chart)	NOTE Where there are 2 or 3 letters, 2 or 3 strands of yarn are used, i.e. 'CD' means one strand each of C and D.
■ = BB	
▲ = CC	
⊠ = CD	
◉ = EE	
☑ = FF	
⊟ = GG	
⊠ = DD	

sleeve (64sts)

LLL
AO
JO
JJ
IJ
HJ
LMN
SS
MMS
MMM
LLM
LLL
LLO
Q
AA
NN
JJ
LLL
Q
JL
LLL
AN
AL
AJ

centre st
back (127sts)
background colours (rep background rows 1-72 to shoulder)

usually try to knit coloured stripes in the rib to echo the richness of the main work.

YARNS FOR TURKISH CARNATION JACKET

Average yarn weight used – 2 strands of lightweight double knitting (sport) or 1 strand of chunky (bulky)

Rowan *Lightweight DK* in the foll 9 colours:

A (#94) grape – 125g (4½oz)
B (#501) hyacinth – 75g (2¾oz)
C (#51) deep sky – 100g (3½oz)
D (#63) powder blue – 375g (13½oz)
E (#35) olive – 25g (1oz)
F (#34) light olive – 25g (1oz)
G (#33) pale lime – 75g (2¾oz)
H (#407) khaki – 25g (1oz)
I (#71) red brown – 25g (1oz)

Rowan *Fine Cotton Chenille* in the foll colour:

J (#385) cyclamen – 150g (5½oz)

Rowan Light Tweed in the foll 2 colours:

L (#216) cherrymix – 275g (10oz)

M (#212) jungle – 50g (1¾oz)

Rowan *Mulberry Silk* in the foll 2 colours:

N (#877) peony – 50g (1¾oz)

O (#874) russett – 50g (1¾oz)

Rowan *Rowanspun Tweed* in the foll 2 colours:

Q (#753) cranberry – 100g (3½oz)

R (#755) damson – 100g (3½oz)

Rowan *Silkstones* in the foll colour:

S (#831) orchid – 50g (1¾oz)

NEEDLES AND NOTIONS

One pair each of 4½mm (US size 7) and 5½mm (US size 9) needles
One 4½mm (US size 7) and one 5½mm (US size 9) circular needle 100cm (39″) long *or size to obtain correct tension (gauge)*
5 buttons

SIZE AND MEASUREMENTS

One size to fit up to 107cm (42″) bust
Actual width across back 71cm (28¼″)
Length to shoulder, including ribbing 76cm (30¼″)
Sleeve length from underarm, including ribbing 43cm (17″)

TENSION (GAUGE)

18 sts and 21 rows to 10cm (4″) over colour patt on 5½mm (US size 9) needles
Check your tension (gauge) before beginning.

NOTES

Do not carry yarns for carnations across back of work, but use a separate length of each colour for each carnation, twisting yarns when changing colours to avoid holes. Carry yarn for background stripes across each row, weaving it around working yarn when not in use.

For both RS (knit) and WS (purl) rows of back read chart from right to left until centre st has been completed, then skipping centre st read chart from left to right across same row for other half of back. For right front read chart from right to left for RS (knit) rows and from left to right for WS (purl) rows. For left front read chart from left to right for RS (knit) rows and

from right to left for WS (purl) rows.

Use 1 strand of yarn where there is only one letter to represent the colour, 2 strands of yarn where there are two letters and 3 strands of yarn where there are three letters, i.e. 'LLM' means 2 strands of L and 1 strand of M.

BACK, FRONTS AND SLEEVES

Back, fronts and sleeves are worked in one piece, beg at lower back edge.

BACK

Using 5½mm (US size 9) circular needle and LLL, cast on 127 sts.

Using AJ, working back and forth in rows and beg with a K row, work 2 rows in st st.

Beg with a K row, cont in st st foll chart from 3rd chart row, working background colours as indicated at left side of chart until 90th chart row has been completed, so ending with a WS row (see Notes for reading chart). Set aside back.

SLEEVES

Using size 5½mm (US size 9) needles and separate length of JL, cast on 64 sts. Break off yarns and slip sts onto a spare needle.

Return to back sts and using JL, cast on 64 sts at beg of next row, then keeping patt correct (91st chart row), work across 64 sts just cast on for right sleeve, 127 sts of back and 64 cast-on sts on spare needle for left sleeve. 255 sts.

Cont in colour patt foll chart until 144th chart row has been completed, so ending with a WS row.

Left: There are several examples in the V&A of this classic stylized carnation.

NECK SHAPING

Divide for back neck and fronts on next row as foll:

145th chart row (RS) Patt 113 sts, cast (bind) off 29 centre sts, patt to end. 113 sts at each side of neck.

146th chart row Patt to neck edge, slip rem sts (right front) on to a spare needle (see foll Note).

Note *If desired work both fronts at same time with separate balls of yarn.*

LEFT FRONT

Cont in colour patt foll chart, AND AT THE SAME TIME shape neck by inc 1 st at neck edge on 153rd chart row and then inc 1 st at neck edge on every 6th row until 198th chart row has been completed, so ending with a WS row.

LEFT SLEEVE SHAPING

199th chart row (RS) Patt to last 64 sts, then using separate length of JL, cast (bind) off rem 64 sts.

**Cont in colour patt foll chart, AND AT THE SAME TIME cont to inc 1 st at neck edge on every 6th row until there are 64 sts. Work in patt without shaping until 288th chart row has been completed.

Using LLL, cast (bind) off.**

RIGHT FRONT

With WS facing, rejoin yarn to neck edge of sts at other side of neck and work as for left front from * to *.

RIGHT SLEEVE SHAPING

Cast (bind) off 64 sts at beg of next row. Complete as for left front from ** to **.

CUFFS

Press back and fronts lightly on WS with a warm iron over a damp cloth.

Using 4½mm (US size 7) needles and LLL and with RS facing, pick up and K70 sts evenly across lower sleeve edge (approx 2 sts for every 3 row ends).

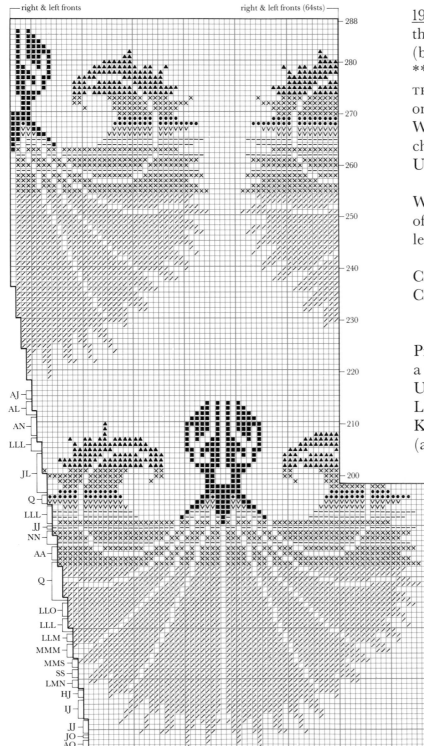

— right & left fronts

right & left fronts (64sts) —

AJ AL AN LLL JL Q LLL JJ NN AA Q LLO LLL LLM MMM MMS SS LMN HJ IJ JJ JO AO LLL

— background colours (rep background rows 145-216 to last row)

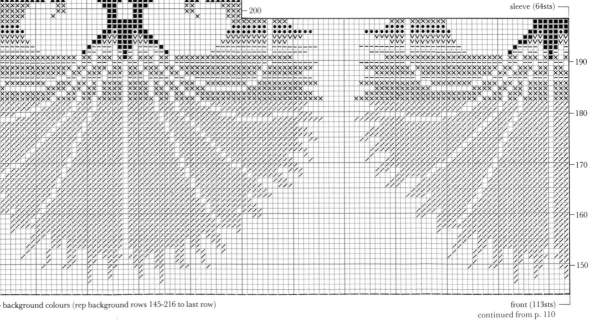

sleeve (64sts) —

front (113sts) —

continued from p. 110

Beg rib on next row as foll:

<u>1st rib row</u> (WS) P1, (K2, P1) to end.

<u>2nd rib row</u> (RS) K1, (P2 tog, K1) to end. 47 sts.

<u>3rd rib row</u> P1, (K1, P1) to end.

<u>4th rib row</u> K1, (P1, K1) to end.

3rd and 4th rows form rib patt and are rep throughout.

Cont in rib, work 4 rows Q, 3 rows LLL, 1 row BB, 2 rows AA and 3 rows Q. Using Q, cast (bind) off tightly in rib.

LOWER BAND

Join side and sleeve seams, using backstitch for st st and invisible seam for ribbing.

Using 4½mm (US size 7) needles and LLL and with RS facing, pick up and K48 sts evenly across lower edge of left front (approx 3 sts for every 4 sts), 101 sts across lower back edge (approx 4 sts for every 5 sts) and 48 sts across right front. 197 sts.

Beg rib as foll:

<u>1st rib row</u> (WS) As 3rd rib row of cuffs.

<u>2nd rib row</u> As 4th rib row of cuffs.

First and 2nd rows form rib patt.

Work 2 rows more in rib.

Complete as for cuffs from *** to ***.

BUTTON BAND

Using 4½mm (US size 7) needles and LLL and with RS facing, pick up and K41 sts evenly along straight centre edge of left front (after neck shaping) to rib (approx 4 sts for every 5 rows ends), then pick up and K13 sts evenly along rib (approx 3 sts for every 2 row ends). 54 sts. Beg with a P row, work 3 rows in st st. Purl 2 rows to form hemline. Beg with a K row, work 4 rows in st st. Cast (bind) off loosely.

BUTTONHOLE BAND

Beg at lower edge of right front, pick up 54 sts along centre edge of right front as for button band. Work buttonholes on next 2 rows as foll:

<u>Next row</u> (WS) P2, *cast (bind) off 2 sts, P10 including st already on needle, rep from * 3 times more, cast (bind) off 2 sts, P2 including st already on needle.

<u>Next row</u> Knit, casting on 2 sts over those cast (bound) off in last row.

Purl 3 rows to form hemline.

Work buttonholes on next 2 rows as foll:

<u>Next row</u> (RS) K2, *cast (bind) off 2 sts, K10 including st already on needle, rep from * 3 times more, cast (bind) off 2 sts, K2 including st already on needle.

<u>Next row</u> (WS) Purl, casting on 2 sts over those cast (bound) off in last row.

Beg with a K row, work 2 rows in st st. Cast (bind) off loosely.

FRONT BAND AND COLLAR

Using 4½mm (US size 7) circular needle and LLL, cast on 271 sts.

Working back and forth in rows, beg rib as foll:

<u>1st rib row</u> Using BB, P1, (K1, P1) to end.

<u>2nd rib row</u> Using BB, K1, (P1, K1) to end.

First and 2nd rows form rib patt.

Using SS, work 2 rows in rib.

COLLAR SHAPING

Keeping rib patt correct, cast (bind) off 6 sts at beg of next row 38 rows, AND AT THE SAME TIME work in stripes as foll:

1 row SS, 2 rows R, 1 row LLO, 1 row R, 2 rows AA, 1 row AN, 2 rows R, 3 rows LLO, 10 rows R, 1 row SS, 1 row BB, 4 rows R, 3 rows LLL, 2 rows AA, 4 rows R. Using R, cast (bind) off rem 43 sts loosely in rib.

FINISHING

Using backstitch, join shaped edge of front band and collar to shaped edge of fronts and back neck. Fold buttonhole and button bands to WS along hemlines and slipstitch in place. Slipstitch ends of buttonhole and button bands to ends of front band.

Press seams lightly on WS with a warm iron over a damp cloth, omitting ribbing. Sew on buttons to correspond with buttonholes. Neaten buttonholes if desired by sewing inside and outside together.

FLOWER INSPIRATIONS

Flowers often dazzle us with their multi-layered complexity. Great curling, rotund petals with blushes of colour look

impossible for any but the cleverest artist to capture on paper. Thankfully this is not true, and the history of decoration is studded with delightful renditions of flowers which are as simple and easy to achieve as a child's drawing. Once you have drawn each shaped petal, no matter how crudely, all you have to do is add a touch of shading to the appropriate corners and, bingo, you have a flower!

Working from painted flowers on china or stitched ones in embroidery is easier, because they have already been abstracted and simplified. Particularly useful are primitive or naive decorative flowers, which are often oversimplified but give you a form which you can embellish with your own colours.

Looking at the sources in the V&A, it is quite thrilling to see how many vari-

Right and above: Flamboyant painted floral richness from the V&A.

Top right: The Flower Trellis carpet is my most ambitious needlepoint kit, containing more than twenty colours.

ations and colour moods can be derived from a few basic flower shapes. The full-blown rose is most common in pinks, oranges and reds. Pure single flowers, like those on the Face Bower vase (page 129), are very easy to achieve, as you can see in the needlepoint cushion adapted from it. Changing the colour of these flowers even slightly gives you many differing effects – for instance adding two-colour centres randomly.

CHINESE ROSE JACKET
Leafing through books on Oriental carpets can reap rich rewards for the textile

115

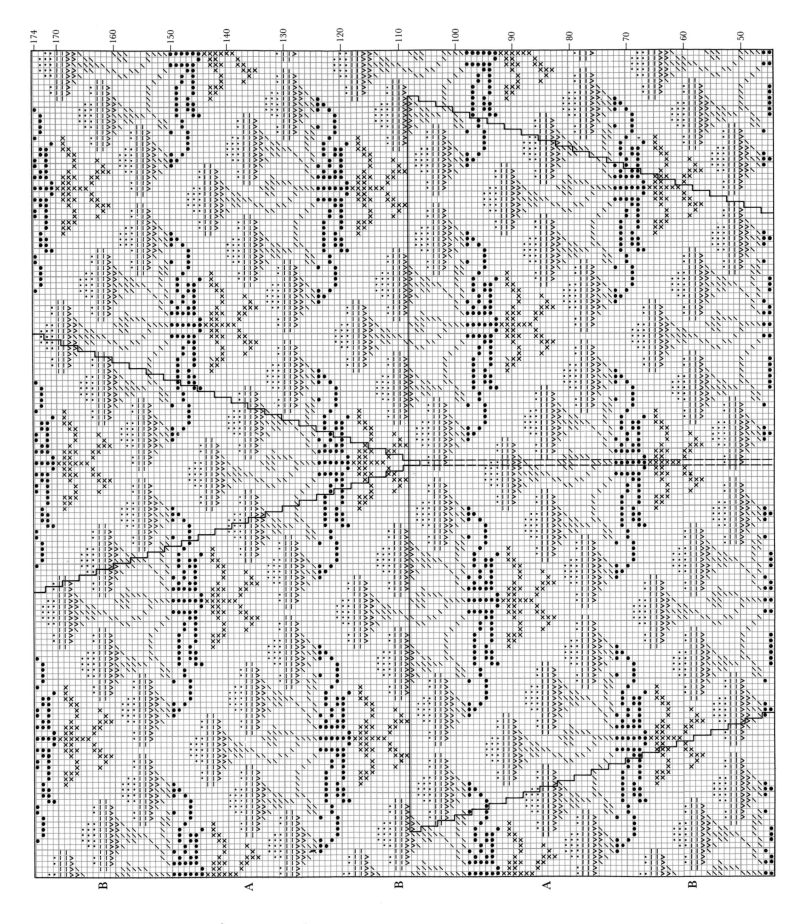

FLOWER 'A'
□ = A
⊠ = G
■ = B
⬛ = C
◩ = D
▣ = H
▤ = J

FLOWER 'B'
□ = A
⊠ = G
● = B
⬛ = C
◩ = E
▣ = L
▤ = F

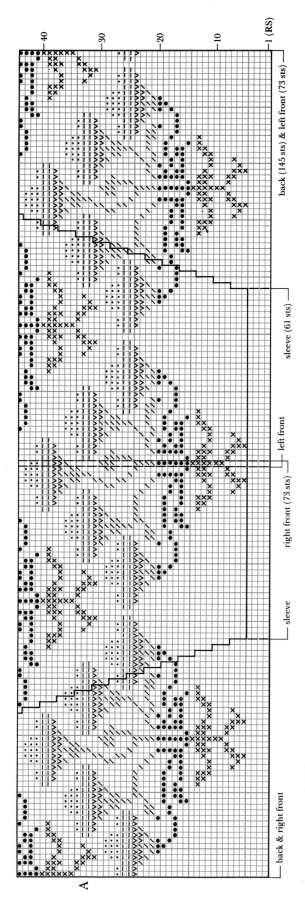

40
30
20
10
1 (RS)

back (145 sts) & left front (73 sts)

sleeve (61 sts)

left front

right front (73 sts)

sleeve

back & right front

A

designer in search of a vehicle for colour. Many of them are limited in colour, however, so always expand whatever colour you see. You know my mottoes: 'When in doubt use twenty more colours!' and 'Anything worth doing is worth overdoing'.

The sprays of flowers on the Chinese Rose jacket and coat are interpreted from an eighteenth-century Mughal carpet. The original has much more detail, with four different clumps of blooms staggered across the rows. Putting that much more variety of shape and colour into a garment would be well worth the effort. It certainly can be done in knitting, as you can see, but is a little easier to do in finer detail in needlepoint. Two of my needlepoint cushions use a Mughal carpet as inspiration.

One of the things that constantly fascinate me about knitting from a chart is the changes in scale that can be achieved by using different-size yarns and needles. For the coat (for shape see Jug coat, page 144), I used chunky-weight yarns and 6½mm (US size 10½) needles and followed the Chinese Rose jacket chart given here. The result was a great, textured, bold coat, containing mohair, ribbons, silk, wool bouclés and cotton slubs. Using three colours a row all over it results in quite a weighty coat – like a fur! Do have a go; or better still, make up your own chart from a favourite carpet, and knit a great coat.

Left: The chart of the Chinese Rose jacket can be used to produce a full-length coat (page 116) the same shape as the Jug coat (pages 144-145).

YARNS FOR CHINESE ROSE JACKET

Yarn weight used – double knitting (knitting worsted)

Rowan *Fleck DK* in the foll 6 colours:
  A (#62F) black – 550g (19½oz)
  B (#51F) deep sky – 100g (3½oz)
  C (#64F) light grey – 100g (3½oz)
  D (#56F) dark blue – 50g (1¾oz)
  E (#77F) rust – 50g (1¾oz)
  F (#410F) pink – 50g (1¾oz)
Rowan *Designer DK* in the foll 4 colours:
  G (#89) pale jade – 50g (1¾oz)
  H (#127) purple – 50g (1¾oz)
  J (#121) lilac – 50g (1¾oz)
  L (#93) dark pink – 50g (1¾oz)

NEEDLES AND NOTIONS

One pair each of 3¼mm (US size 3), 3¾mm (US size 5) and 4mm (US size 6) needles *or size to obtain correct tension (gauge)*
7 buttons

SIZE AND MEASUREMENTS

One size to fit up to 107cm (42″) bust
Actual width across back 60cm (24″)
Length to shoulder 66cm (26½″)
Sleeve length 41cm (16½″)

TENSION (GAUGE)

24 sts and 27 rows to 10cm (4″) over colour patt on 4mm (US size 6) needles
Check your tension (gauge) before beginning.

NOTES

When using two or more colours in a row, carry colour not in use loosely across back of work, weaving it around working yarn on every 3rd st. Read chart from right to left for RS (knit) rows and from left to right for WS (purl) rows.

BACK

Using 3¾mm (US size 5) needles and A, cast on 145 sts. Beg moss st patt as foll:
1st row (K1, P1) to last st, K1.
Rep last row 4 times more.
Change to 4mm (US size 6) needles and beg with a K row, work 4 rows in st st.
Beg with a K row, cont in st st foll chart from 5th chart row, working each row of flowers in colour sequence for flower 'A' or flower 'B' as indicated until 102nd chart row has been completed.
Mark last row for position of armholes.
Cont in colour patt foll chart until 174th chart row has been completed.
Cast (bind) off.

POCKET LININGS

Using 4mm (US size 6) needles and A, cast on 29 sts. Beg with a K row, work 34 rows in st st. Leave sts on a spare needle.

FRONTS

Note *If desired, work both fronts at same time with separate balls of yarn.*
Using 3¾mm (US size 5) needles and A, cast on 73 sts. Work 5 rows in moss st patt as for back.
Change to 4mm (US size 6) needles and beg with a K row, work 4 rows in st st.
Beg with a K row, cont in st st foll chart from 5th chart row, working each row of flowers in colour sequence for flower 'A' or flower 'B' as indicated until 50th chart row has been completed. Work pocket opening for left or right front as foll:

LEFT FRONT POCKET OPENING
51st row Patt 12 sts, slip next 29 sts onto a stitch holder and in place of these sts patt across 29 sts of pocket lining from spare needle, patt across rem sts of front.

RIGHT FRONT POCKET OPENING
51st row Patt 32 sts, slip next 29 sts onto a st holder and in place of these sts patt across 29 sts of pocket lining from spare needle, patt across rem sts of front.

LEFT AND RIGHT FRONTS
Cont in colour patt foll chart until 106th chart row has been completed (marking 102nd row for position of armholes), so ending with a WS row.

NECK SHAPING
Cont in colour patt foll chart until 173rd chart row has been completed, AND AT THE SAME TIME dec 1 st at neck edge on next row and then on every 3rd row until 50 sts rem.
Work 174th chart row. Cast (bind) off.

SLEEVES

Note *If desired, work both sleeves at same time with separate balls of yarn.*

Using 3¾mm (US size 5) needles and A, cast on 61 sts.

Work 5 rows in moss st patt as for back. Change to 4mm (US size 6) needles and beg with a K row, cont in st st foll chart from 5th chart row (omitting first 4 chart rows of st st), working each row of flowers in colour sequence for flower 'A' or flower 'B' as indicated until 107th chart row has been completed, AND AT THE SAME TIME shape sleeve by inc 1 st at each end of 4th row and then every 3rd row until there are 129 sts.

Work 1 row more in patt, or work until sleeve is required length. Cast (bind) off loosely.

POCKET TOPS

Pocket tops are worked in st st in charted colour patt for 5 rows, then a fold-over hem is added.

LEFT FRONT

Using 3¼mm (US size 3) needles, slip left front pocket opening sts from stitch holder onto left-hand needle and with RS facing, extend colour patt as foll:

1st row K1A, (13L, 1A) twice.
2nd row P1A, (13L, 1A) twice.
3rd row K2A, *2F, 1A, 5F, 1A, 2F*, 3A, rep from * to * once more, 2A.
4th row P5A, 5F, 9A, 5F, 5A.
5th row K6A, 3F, 11A, 3F, 6A.

Cont with A only, purl 1 row. Knit 2 rows to form hemline.
Beg with a K row, work 6 rows in st st. Cast (bind off).

RIGHT FRONT

Work as for left front pocket top, but working 5 colour patt rows as foll:

1st row K5A, 13L, 1A, 10L.
2nd row P10L, 1A, 13L, 5A.
3rd row K6A, *2F, 1A, 5F, 1A*, 2F, 3A, rep from * to * once more.
4th row P1A, (5F, 9A) twice.
5th row K10A, 3F, 11A, 3F, 2A.

LEFT FRONT BAND AND COLLAR

Press all pieces lightly on WS with a warm iron over a damp cloth.
Using backstitch, join shoulder seams.
Beg button band as foll:

Using 3¾mm (US size 5) needles and A, cast on 6 sts.

Beg moss st patt as foll:
1st row (K1, P1) to end.
2nd row (P1, K1) to end.
Last 2 rows form moss st patt.

Work in moss st patt until band, when slightly stretched, fits up front to first front neck dec, ending with a WS row.
Keeping moss st patt correct, inc 1 st at beg of next row and then at same edge on every 4th row until there are 30 sts.
Cont in moss st patt without shaping until band fits up front to centre back neck.
Cast (bind) off in moss st patt.

Mark positions of 7 buttons on left front band, the first 2.5cm (1″) from cast on edge, the last 2.5cm (1″) down from beg of neck shaping and the rem 5 buttons evenly spaced between.

RIGHT FRONT BAND AND COLLAR

Using 3¾mm (US size 5) needles and A, cast on 6 sts.

Work as for left front band, reversing shaping and making buttonholes to correspond with positions of buttons as foll:

1st buttonhole row Patt 2 sts, cast (bind) off 2 sts, patt to end.
2nd buttonhole row Patt to end, casting on 2 sts over those cast (bound) off.

FINISHING

Using backstitch, join cast (bound) off edge of sleeves to back and fronts between markers, matching centre of top of sleeve to shoulder seam. Using backstitch, join side and sleeve seams.

Pin left front band (button band) and collar to left front and sew in place. Join right front band (buttonhole band) and collar to right front in the same way. Join collar seam.

Slipstitch pocket linings to WS of fronts. Fold each pocket hem to WS along hemline and slipstitch in place. Sew side edges of pocket tops to RS. Press seams lightly on WS with a warm iron over a damp cloth. Sew on buttons to correspond with buttonholes.

Right and below right: Here are the Cauliflower and Cabbage cushion kits adapted for use as placemats.

Opposite page: Steve's use of trailing foxgloves gives this still life a vigorous, leafy energy. I have always coveted the Staffordshire cauliflower tea set from the V&A.

FRUITS AND VEGETABLES

Anyone who grows vegetables or fruit attains an insight into their amazing beauty. One follows a tender plant or tree through its early growth, on to buds and blossoms which give way to green fruit that slowly acquire blushes of colour, and through to harvest.

As a child, I had a little vegetable patch on the wild coast of California. Growing courgettes (I called them zucchini) and pumpkins and Indian corn was a thrill. The huge orange trumpet flowers of the courgettes and the white silk and varied colours in the corn set my child's imagination soaring. The Indian corn was the multi-coloured kind of maize which grows in shades of maroon, blue, white and gold. Within a single ear of corn you can perceive endless shades of colours.

I am quite certain that my love of colour toning stems from such early experiences. My grandmother had an orchard up in the Carmel Valley, and the sight of trees burgeoning with pinky-orange apricots against a vivid blue sky

was heaven on earth.

Given this background, it is not surprising that the eighteenth-century Staffordshire cauliflower tea set in the V&A always caught my eye when I visited the museum. It was just a matter of time until it made me take a fresh look at the humble cauliflower. The cauliflower to me is such a wonderfully flamboyant shape that I could even see it as a bridal bouquet! Steve's still life of my needle-

point and the tea set is one of my favourites in the book.

MELON TAPESTRY

The Melon tapestry could be entitled 'spheres with slices'. The lush round shapes of melons, especially with ridges and stripes to emphasize the roundness,

are delicious. Leaves, apples and pears seemed a good counterbalancing framework, nestled in around these generous shapes. The warm beige comes from the border of the melon plate (below left). I was going to incorporate the baroque lace as a border, because I like that fresh white-on-beige look, but thought white dots would serve the same end.

It was quite a temptation at first to go dark and rich with this piece, but Steve encouraged me to keep a light, frothy watercolour-feel in the composition. That leaves the deep shadows and the touches of dark reds as dramatic corners to contrast with the glowing light of the fruit. The central melon, with its peachy interior, is a direct quote from the melon plate (below left).

You will notice that I have used three or four shades of beige in the background and two or three shades of creamy white. These changes give depth, or movement, to an otherwise static ground.

Interpreting subjects, like this fruit, at larger-than-life scale is really exciting and allows you to include every detail you can perceive in your source material. I often admire the exaggerated fruit and vegetable portraits in medieval and Elizabethan embroideries. They are very instructive in their simplified, bold scale. I love the way each leaf is defined, even in the summer foliage of a huge tree. This naive approach gives me courage to draw my subjects boldly.

Opposite page: I used several details from this boldly painted plate in the Melon tapestry.

This page: Some of the delightful vegetable and fruit fantasies among the V&A's porcelains (left) and Melon tapestry in progress (below).

*Right: The Melon
tapestry with some of
its real-life models.*

FAUNA AND FOLLIES

A bizarre image that caught my eye on an early visit to London's Portobello Market was a cabbage teapot with a snake crawling through it to form the spout and handle. Later, in antique shops and museums, including the V&A, I came across hundreds of objects, such as boxes, spoons, jars and bells, that disguised themselves as something quite fanciful. The melon and fish tureens (page 125) are a case in point. I am delighted by this sort of whimsical humour in decoration and enjoy adding to this collection of ideas.

Needlepoint is an ideal medium in which to create illusionary objects. Shell and fan lampshades and duck, cat and face cushions are only some of the many ideas I have toyed with in this genre.

The V&A and other great collections of decorative art are peppered with amusing and beautifully fashioned objects that – like the enamel snuffbox heads in the V&A (page 134) – make very jolly subjects for needlepoint. I particularly like working from subjects in the natural world, such as animals, insects and shells (page 10), taking ideas of interpretation from the past. The museum objects that have stood the test of time often exemplify the use of a refined colour and rendering which can make our contemporary furnishings more deeply beautiful.

Right: There is quite a magical feel about these pale little faces appearing in the flowers. The delicate turbaned lady in porcelain is one of my favourites in the V&A's collection of pipes.

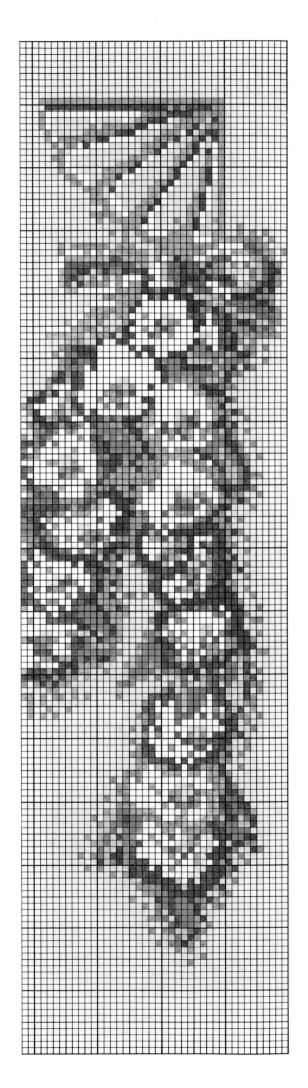

FACE BOWER CUSHION

These pristine white faces, surrounded by flowers on a lemon yellow background, captured my attention on every visit to the V&A, until I had to do something about it! This needlepoint cushion should light up a corner of any room.

There is something about these tall vases, with their strong, serious faces framed by the delicate cascades of flowers, that really moves me. The expanse of bold yellow gives the whole design quite a strong glow. I have always loved the way faces have been used for decoration, from magical old merry-go-rounds to carvings in architecture. These faces and flowers would make an attractive chair back and, at the same time, create a very sunny effect.

MATERIALS FOR FACE BOWER CUSHION

Appleton *tapestry wool* in the following 12 colours and approximate amounts:

423 (16m/17yd)		743 (11m/12yd)
874 (8m/9yd)		461 (14m/15yd)
753 (8m/9yd)		184 (22m/24yd)
707 (10m/11yd)		844 (29m/31yd)
862 (7m/8yd)		551 (201m/220yd)
885 (7m/8yd)		991 (45m/49yd)

10-mesh double-thread or interlocked canvas 52cm (20½") square
90cm (1yd) of 90cm (36") wide backing fabric and matching thread
31cm (12") zipper
1.7m (2yd) of piping (filler) cord

*Pages 130 and 131:
The Face Bower
cushion in progress.
You will see that I
tried it first in a
softer creamy yellow
and sharper flower
colours.*

*Overleaf: Keeping
company with my
Stone Head
needlepoint is a
wonderful motley
crowd of varied faces
which inhabit the
vessels, textiles and
paintings in the
V&A. These
particular sources are
from Elizabethan
miniatures, Tibetan
embroidery,
enamelled snuffboxes
and china pots.*

*Left: Close-up of the
Face Bower cushion.*

Far right: Laughing Buddhas are a happy talisman for my life. Here they make good companions for the Snuffbox cushion.

Finished needlepoint measures approximately 42cm (16½") by 41cm (16¼")

WORKING FACE BOWER CUSHION

The chart is 164 stitches wide by 162 stitches high. Work the embroidery onto the canvas and block the finished needlepoint as for Fish placemat (page 145) from * to * and from ** to **. ***Cover the piping cord with bias strips of the lining fabric and baste it to the edge of the needlepoint. Cut the lining to the same size as the finished needlepoint plus 1.5cm (½") extra all around for the seam allowance, after having inserted the zipper in the centre. With the right sides facing, sew the lining to the needlepoint, catching in the piping, and turn the cushion cover right side out. Press the seams lightly with the needlepoint face down.***

Top right: My watercolour sketch for the Snuffbox cushion.

Bottom right: The radiating stripes in Victorian circus colours made a good ground and design for my Snuffbox Heads needlepoint.

This page and opposite page: Birds and fish are represented delightfully in the various decorative disciplines to be found in the V&A. The Duck needlepoint cushions and the fish watercolour are a mere beginning of my exploration of this charming theme.

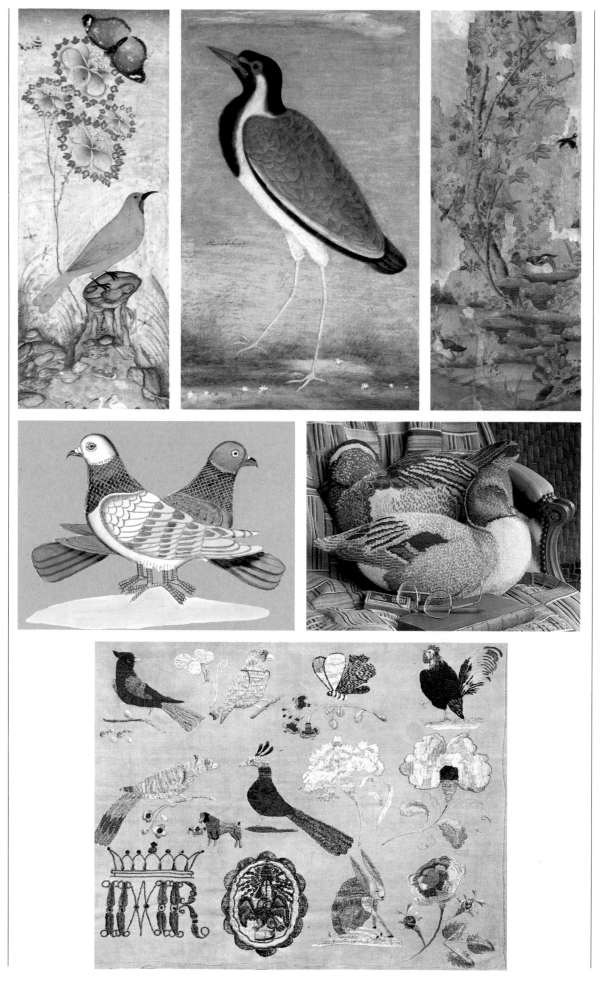

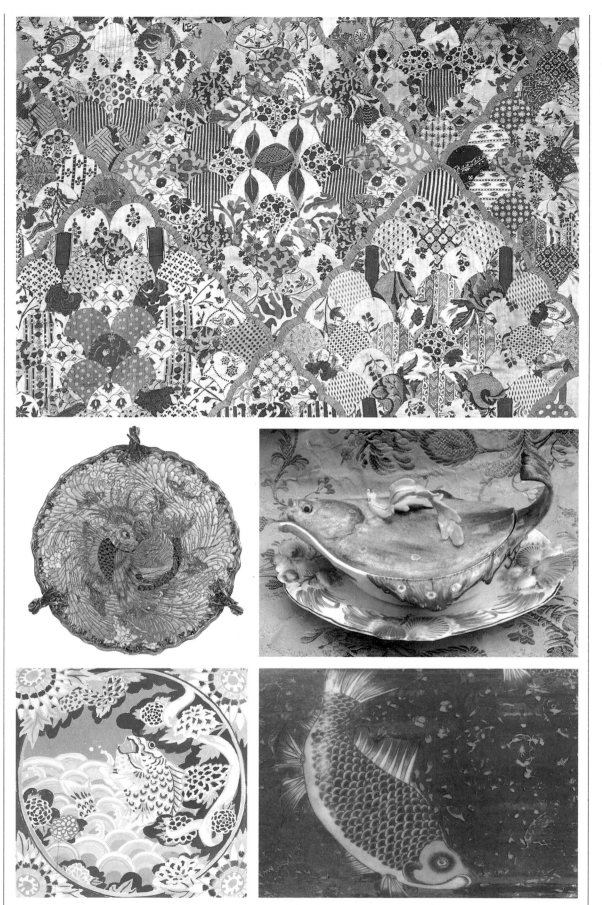

*Overleaf: The Fish
placemat seen with
the eighteenth-century
'Delftware' dish that
inspired it and others
of the same school of
decoration.*

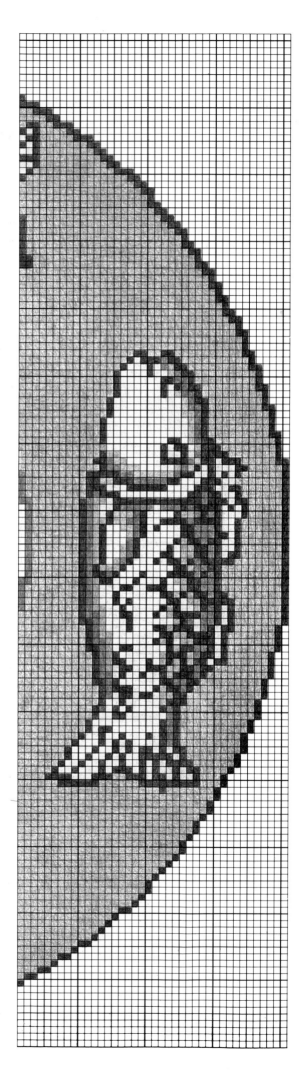

FISH PLACEMAT

So often, in a huge assortment of decorative objects, a good design practically leaps off the shelf at you. Steve spotted a simple fish plate in the V&A and urged me to design a placemat using this motif.

It was very enjoyable to stitch the bold fish on their speckled ground. I felt that a big shell was stronger for the centre than the landscape detail on the actual plate.

The eighteenth-century English imitation Delftware, which was the source for this design, has always attracted me with its variations in mulberry coloured grounds. Several of these plates (pages 140 and 141) would make handsome needlepoint subjects. Needlepoint is also a good medium for portraying highly detailed fish, and I want to explore that one day.

MATERIALS FOR FISH PLACEMAT

Appleton *tapestry wool* in the following 5 colours and approximate amounts:

- ■ 925 (17m/18yd) ▨ 876 (47m/51yd)
- ▨ 743 (20m/22yd) ▨ 126 (8m/9yd)
- ▨ 461 (11m/12yd)

Appleton *crewel wool* in the following 3 colours and approximate amounts:

- ▨ 712 (114m/124yd) □ 992 (160m/174yd)
- ▨ 988 (137m/149yd)

10-mesh double-thread or interlocked canvas 48cm (19″) square
52cm (20″) square piece of felt backing
Finished needlepoint measures approximately 38cm (15″) in diameter

Left: These simple, primitive fish could be placed on any number of coloured grounds.

WORKING FISH PLACEMAT

The chart is 151 stitches in diameter. *Count the canvas threads to mark the width and height of the diameter of the needlepoint onto the canvas. Make a template of the canvas outline by tracing the outline on the canvas onto a piece of paper or by cutting a piece of paper the same size as the outline. Set aside to use later to block the finished needlepoint. Following the chart, work the embroidery in tent stitch using *one strand* of tapestry wool* for all of the colours except the backgrounds of the inner and outer circles. For the background of the outer circle use *three strands* of crewel wool together – one strand each of 712, 988 and 992. For the background of the inner circle use three strands of crewel wool together – one strand of 988 and 2 strands of 992. **Block the finished needlepoint by dampening it on the wrong side, pinning it out to the correct size following the paper template and leaving it to dry. Trim the canvas around the needlepoint.** Clip the edge, turn to wrong side and press. Cut the felt the same size as the finished needlepoint and sew to the back of the placemat.

JUG COAT

I have always been attracted to china pots, and particularly to blue and white ones. They seemed complicated to depict in textiles until I began to come across Chinese paintings of them done in a sim-

Left: Classic blue and white china provided fresh subject matter for this knitted Jug coat, shot against an English barn covered with old textile wood blocks.

Below: These are just a few of the hundreds of superb blue and white pots to work from in the V&A collection.

plified, flat manner. Then I saw that many other cultures treat blue and white wonderfully in this flat style. Turkish wall decorations, Indian and Russian miniatures, tiles, carpets and embroideries from all over the world include these simple, easy-to-read representations of blue and white pots, often with great bouquets of flowers. My first needlepoint kit design for Ehrman (called Caucasian Flower needlepoint cushion cover) used a blue and white vase with flowers inspired by stencilled painting on an Afghan truck.

It was just a matter of time before I knitted some jolly blue and white jug designs, and this coat is my first attempt. I am sure you can think of many other projects to try. With this design I simply drew the pot shapes on graph paper and filled in each one with easy-to-knit geometric or floral motifs.

I then placed these clear-cut motifs on grounds of marble-like tweed. I gathered about fifty shades of pinky-beiges, browns, grey-blues, greens and lavenders. The pots have about ten shades of cream, pale green or blue in them, with ten shades of deep blue for the decorations. There is no stark white, so that the allover impression is rather antique and muted. The main objective is a soft richness. Each square is gently distinct in its toning, without being too contrasting. Groups of greeny-greys sit next to browny-greys, next to lavender-greys.

Right: You can see here in the Jug coat the various striped tones in the ground and the subtly different shades of cream and blue.

Some pots are in bright blue marlings or mixtures; others in navy or tweedy air force blue. Using combinations of thin yarns will help you to create the marled tweedy mixtures in the squares.

I look forward to seeing the variations that people who also love blue and white will come up with. Think of the many shades of marble you could play with, or – for a very stark coat or jacket – black and white pots with dark grey squares. If the coat is a bit too much for you, make a luxurious wide jacket by just leaving off the bottom two rows of pots and jugs.

YARNS FOR JUG COAT
Average yarn weight used – chunky (bulky)
Approx 1300g (49oz) in a mixture of yarns and colours in medium shades for patch backgrounds A
Approx 450g (16oz) in a mixture of yarns and colours in light shades for jugs B
Approx 350g (13oz) in a mixture of yarns and colours in dark shades for jug motif designs C

NEEDLES
One pair each of 5mm (US size 8) and 6mm (US size 10) needles
One 5mm (US size 8) and one 6mm (US size 10) circular needle 100cm (39″) long
or size to obtain correct tension (gauge)

SIZE AND MEASUREMENTS
One size to fit up to 112cm (44″) bust
Actual width across back 94cm (37½″)
Length to shoulder, including ribbing 116cm (46½″)
Sleeve length from underarm, including ribbing 28cm (11″)

TENSION (GAUGE)
16 sts and 19 rows to 10cm (4″) over colour patt on 6mm (US size 10) needles
Check your tension (gauge) before beginning.

NOTES
Do not carry yarn for patch backgrounds (A) and jugs (B) across entire row, but use a separate length of each colour for each area of colour. Carry yarn for jugs (B) and jug motifs (C) loosely across back of jug when not in use, weav-

ing it around working yarn.
Choose background colour for each patch as desired, but be sure to match front half patches at side seams. Use contrasting colours for all other patches at side seams.
Read chart from right to left for RS (knit) rows and from left to right for WS (purl) rows.

BACK, FRONTS AND SLEEVES

Back, fronts and sleeves are worked in one piece, beg at lower back edge.

BACK

Using 6mm (US size 10) circular needle and A, cast on 150 sts.

Working back and forth in rows, beg colour patt as foll:

Beg with a K row, work in st st foll chart from first chart row and working each patch background in random stripes in a different set of shades of A, until 157th chart row has been completed, so ending with a RS row (see <u>Notes</u> for patch colours). Set aside back.

SLEEVES

Using size 6mm (US size 10) needles and separate length of A, cast on 27 sts for right sleeve. Break off yarn and set aside.

Return to back sts and using A, cast on 27 sts at beg of next row, then keeping patt correct (158th chart row), work across 27 sts just cast on for left sleeve, 150 sts of back and 27 cast-on sts for right sleeve. 204 sts.

Cont in colour patt foll chart until 206th chart row has been completed, so ending with a WS row.

NECK SHAPING

Divide for back neck and fronts on next row as foll:

<u>207th chart row</u> (RS) Patt 94 sts, cast (bind) off 16 centre sts, patt to end. 94 sts at each side of neck.

<u>208th chart row</u> Patt to neck edge, slip rem sts (right front) onto a spare needle (see foll <u>Note</u>).

<u>Note</u> *If desired work both fronts at same time with separate balls of yarn.*

LEFT FRONT

Mark neck edge of last row for shoulder line to indicate position of back neck.

Cont in colour patt on these sts for left front by reading chart downwards beg with 208th chart row and changing patch background colours on next row, AND AT THE SAME TIME cast (bind) off 6 sts at beg of next row (neck edge), dec 1 st at neck edge on foll alternate row, *work 5 rows without shaping, inc 1 st at neck edge on next row, inc 1 st at neck edge on foll alternate row, then cast on at neck edge on every foll alternate row: 2 sts once, 4 sts once and 7 sts once. 102 sts.

Work in patt without shaping, foll chart from centre to cuff edge only, until front sleeve has same number of rows as back sleeve from shoulder line, ending with a RS row.*

LEFT SLEEVE SHAPING

Cast (bind) off 27 sts at beg of next row. 75 sts.

**Work in patt without shaping until first chart row has been completed, so ending with a WS row.

Using same colour as first cast on row, work 1 row and slip all sts onto a spare needle.**

RIGHT FRONT

With WS facing, rejoin yarn to neck edge of sts at other side of neck and cast (bind) off 6 sts, patt to end.

Mark neck edge of last row for shoulder line to indicate position of back neck.

Cont in colour patt on these sts for right front by reading chart downwards beg with 208th chart row and changing patch background colours on next row, AND AT THE SAME TIME work 1 row without shaping, dec 1 st at neck edge on next row, then work as for left front from * to *, but ending with a RS row.

RIGHT SLEEVE SHAPING

<u>Next row</u> (WS) Patt 75 sts, cast (bind) off rem 27 sts.

With RS facing, rejoin yarn and work as for left front from ** to **.

CUFFS

Press back and fronts lightly on WS with a warm iron over a damp cloth.

Using 5mm (US size 8) needles and A and with RS facing, pick up and K49 sts evenly across lower sleeve edge (approx 1 st for every 2 row ends).

Working in random stripes of A through-

□ = A
☑ = B
◉ = C

out, beg rib as foll:
1st rib row (WS) P1, (K2, P1) to end.
2nd rib row (RS) K1, (P2 tog, K1) to end.
33 sts.
3rd rib row P1, (K1, P1) to end.

4th rib row K1, (P1, K1) to end.
3rd and 4th rows form rib patt and are
rep throughout. Cont in rib patt until
cuff measures 11cm (4¼") from beg.
Cast (bind) off tightly in rib.

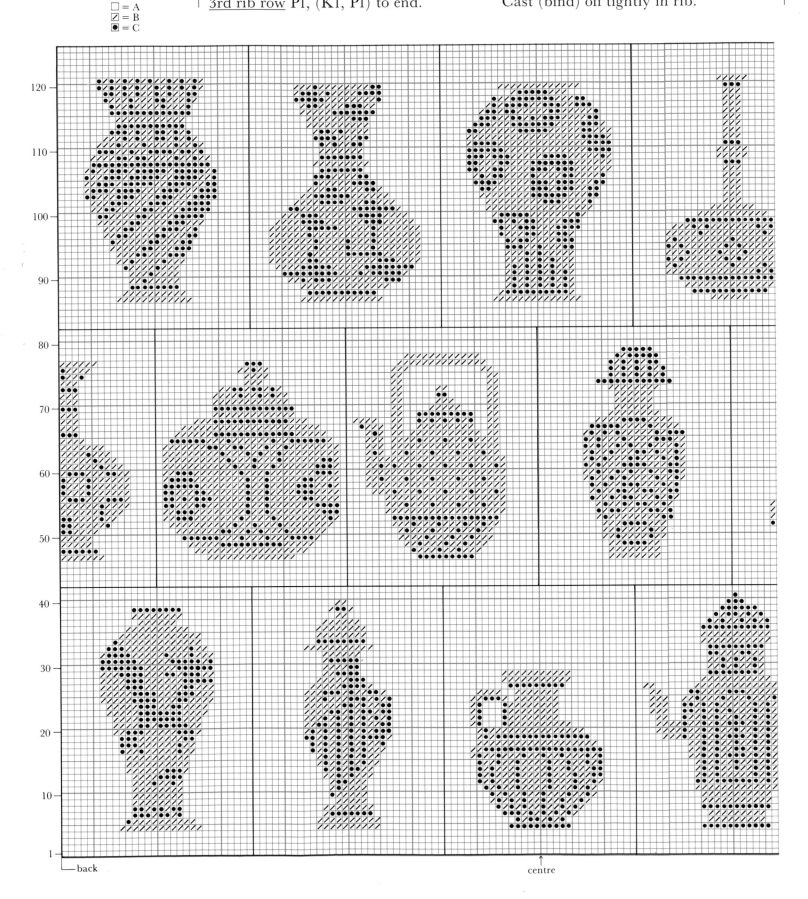

back

centre

RIGHT FRONT POCKET

Using 5mm (US size 8) needles and A
and with RS facing, pick up and K25 sts
evenly along right side-seam edge of back
between 110th and 140th chart rows

continued on next page

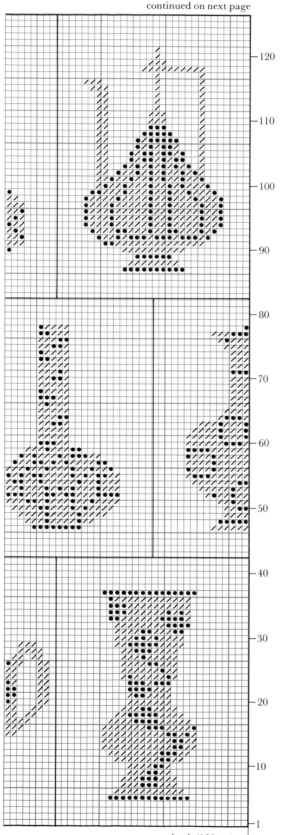

back (150 sts)

(approx 5 sts for every 6 row ends).
Using same shade of A throughout, purl
1 row. Cast on 8 sts at beg of next row and
knit across row. 33 sts.
***Cont in st st, dec 1 st at top edge of
pocket on next row, then dec 1 st at same
edge on every alternate row until 20 sts
rem.
Cast (bind) off loosely.***

LEFT FRONT POCKET

Using 5mm (US size 8) needles and A
and with RS facing, pick up and K25 sts
evenly along left side-seam edge of back
as for right front pocket.
Cast on 8 sts at beg of next row and purl
across row. 33 sts.
Complete as for right front pocket from
*** to ***.

POCKET BANDS

Using 5mm (US size 8) needles and A
and with RS facing, pick up and K25 sts
evenly along right front side-seam edge
at position corresponding with pocket.
Using same shade of A throughout, knit 1
row to form hemline.
Beg with a K row, work in st st for 4 rows
more. Cast (bind) off loosely. Work
pocket band on left front in the same
way.

LOWER BAND

Join side and sleeve seams, leaving pockets open and using backstitch for st st and
invisible seam for ribbing.
Using 5mm (US size 8) circular needle
and A and with RS facing, knit first st at
lower edge of left front from spare needle,
(K2 tog) 37 times across rem sts of left
front, pick up and K77 sts evenly across
lower back edge (approx 1 st for every 2
sts), then (K2 tog) 37 times across lower
edge of right front from spare needle, knit
rem st. 153 sts.
Working back and forth in rows in random stripes of A throughout, beg rib as
foll:
1st rib row (WS) As 3rd rib row of cuffs.
2nd rib row As 4th rib row of cuffs.
First and 2nd rows form rib patt and are
rep throughout. Cont in rib patt until

lower band measures 7cm (2¾″) from beg. Cast (bind) off loosely in rib.

LEFT FRONT BAND

Using 5mm (US size 8) circular needle and A and with RS facing, pick up and K162 sts evenly along centre edge of left front to lower band (approx 5 sts for every 6 row ends), then pick up and K13 sts along ribbed band. 175 sts.

Using same shade of A throughout and working back and forth in rows, knit 1 row to form hemline.

Beg with a K row, work in st st for 10 rows more. Cast (bind) off loosely.

RIGHT FRONT BAND

Using 5mm (US size 8) needles and A and with RS facing, pick up and K175 sts evenly along centre edge of right front. Complete as for left front band.

COLLAR

Fold front bands to WS along hemline and slipstitch in place. Using 5mm (US size 8) needles and A and with RS facing, pick up and K29 sts evenly along right front neck edge, 33 sts across back neck and 29 sts along left front neck edge. 91 sts. Working in random stripes of A throughout, beg rib as foll:

1st rib row (WS) As 3rd rib row of cuffs.

2nd rib row As 4th rib row of cuffs.

Rep first and 2nd rows twice more, then rep first row once.

8th rib row (RS) (K1, P1) 4 times, sl 1-K1-psso, *(K1, P1) 5 times, sl 1-K1-psso, rep from * 5 times more, K1, (P1, K1) to end. 84 sts.

9th rib row (P1, K1) 4 times, P2, *K1, (P1, K1) 4 times, P2, rep from * 5 times more, (K1, P1) to end.

10th rib row (K1, P1) 4 times, K2, *(P1,

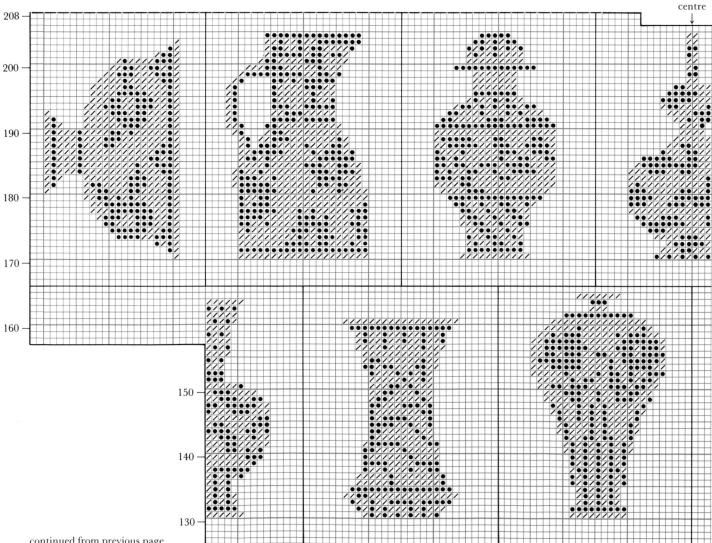

continued from previous page

K1) 4 times, P1, K2, rep from * 5 times
more, (P1, K1) to end.
Rep 9th and 10th rows twice more, then
rep 9th row once.

16th rib row (RS) (K1, P1) 4 times, sl 1-
K1-psso, *(P1, K1) 4 times, P1, sl 1-
K1-psso, rep from * 5 times more, (P1,
K1) to end. 77 sts.

17th rib row P1, (K1, P1) to end.
Cast (bind) off in rib.

FINISHING
Fold pocket bands to WS of fronts along
hemline and slipstitch in place. Slipstitch
pockets carefully to WS of fronts.
Press seams lightly on WS with a warm
iron over a damp cloth, omitting ribbing.

JUG PLATE CUSHION
Like the inspiration for the fish placemat
(page 141), the naive, jaunty plate that
inspired the Jug Plate cushion was a gift
to a designer. The fresh drawings of the
blue and white pots on deep, rich yellow
were easy to capture in needlepoint tent
stitches. The bold impression of these
pots, with their childlike perspective,
made me want to change as little as possible of the original design.

I have put a high green and pink chequerboard behind the plate, but any
colours that suit your furnishings could
be substituted in order to make the
cushion work in your particular scheme.

You could also make a charming
border of blue and white pots around a
carpet, cushion or table mat, using these
shapes lined up in rows instead of placed
on the plate. For more variety, work in
the pots from the Jug coat (page 144).
The V&A abounds with good examples
of blue and white ceramics for you to use

*Overleaf: The yellow
Jug Plate cushion
with the confident
original that inspired
it and some jaunty
blue and white
porcelains from the
V&A.*

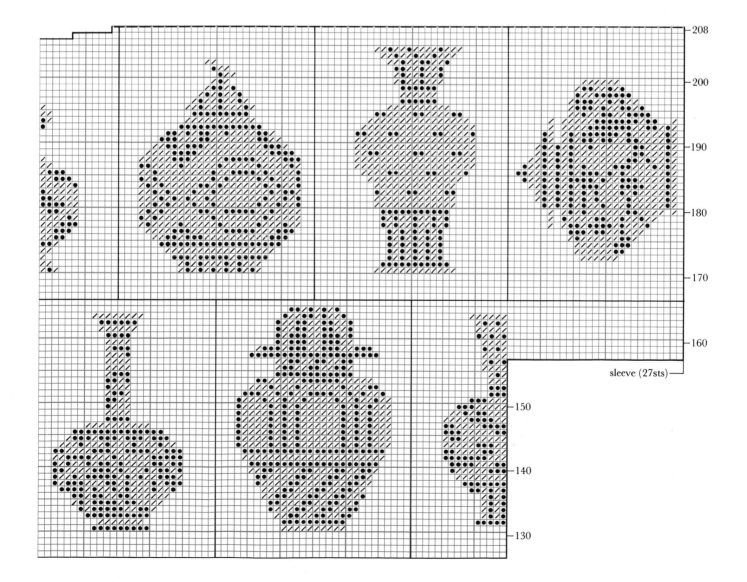

151

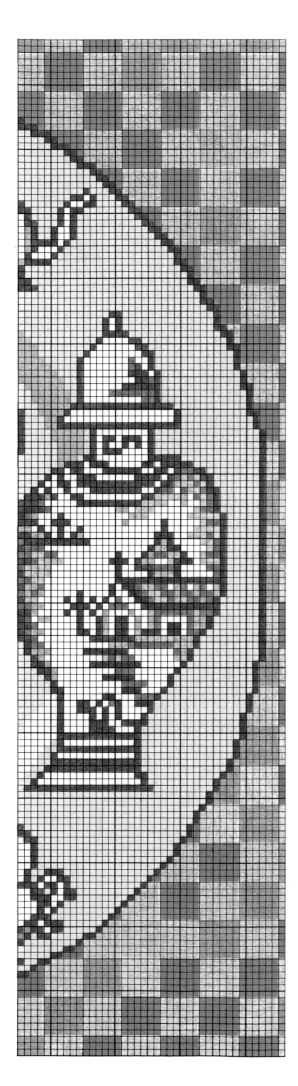

as sources for your own series of pots.

Hugh Ehrman has commissioned me to design a wallpaper of blue and white pots on bright yellow, with a version on a mauve spattered ground, like the 'Delft-ware' (pages 140 and 141) from the V&A. (See page 158 for wallpaper details.)

MATERIALS FOR JUG PLATE CUSHION

Appleton *tapestry wool* in the following 11 colours and approximate amounts:

■	746 (51m/56yd)		872 (6m/6yd)
■	744 (17m/18yd)	■	425 (25m/27yd)
■	461 (18m/20yd)	■	423 (25m/27yd)
■	751 (54m/59yd)		421 (3m/3yd)
■	844 (7m/8yd)	□	992 (51m/56yd)
	552 (95m/104yd)		

10-mesh double-thread or interlocked canvas 50cm (20″) square
90cm (1yd) of 90cm (36″) wide backing fabric and matching thread
31cm (12″) zipper
1.7m (2yd) of piping (filler) cord
Finished needlepoint measures approximately 40cm (15¾″) square

WORKING JUG PLATE CUSHION

The chart is 158 stitches wide by 159 stitches high. Work as for Fish placemat (page 145) from * to * (for a cleaner white look, try pure white 991 instead of off white 992 for the jugs) and from ** to **. Work as for Face Bower cushion (page 136) from *** to ***.

Left: Working from primitive sources, like the pots on the yellow plate, should give the amateur artist courage.

V&A
SOURCES LIST

The following are details for the objects featured which are in the collection of the Victoria and Albert Museum, The National Museum of Art and Design, South Kensington, London SW7 2RL, England. The numbers in parentheses are the museum reference numbers. An asterisk(*) denotes that the photograph is courtesy of the V&A.

PAGE 3
Plate decorated with melon and flowers and painted in enamel colours and gilt, ENGLISH, Coalport, 1820-30, (C.62-1939).

PAGE 8
TOP:
*Gouache or opaque watercolour on paper of a groom holding the reins of a royal horse, INDIAN, Decann, about 1600, (IS.88-1965).
BOTTOM:
*Ceramic harlequin, GERMAN, Meissen, 1740, (C.12-1984).

PAGE 9
TOP:
Porcelain plaque decorated with flowers, ENGLISH, Derby, painted by Horatio Steele, about 1830, (3059-1901).
BOTTOM LEFT:
*Painted satin, ENGLISH, 1860-70, (T.21-1947).
BOTTOM RIGHT:
Detail from porcelain vase, ITALIAN, Capodimonte, about 1750-55, (C.412-1926).

PAGE 10
TOP LEFT:
*Porcelain urn with shell decoration, ENGLISH, Worcester, possibly painted by Thomas Baxter, 1820, (C.511-1935).

PAGE 11
TOP:
*Wooden court fan, JAPAN, 19th century, (T.514-1919).

PAGES 12-13
(Back row left to right)
Small blue earthenware vase, ENGLISH, Pilkingtons, 1904, (CIRC.185-1958).
Large leaf-green earthenware vase with handles, ENGLISH, made for Liberty & Co. by C.H. Branham, early 20th century, (CIRC.339-1965).
Large red earthenware vase, ENGLISH, Pilkingtons, 1905-1913, (187-1958).
Large royal blue earthenware vase, ENGLISH, Bretby Art Pottery,

about 1925, (C.51-1980).
(Front row, left to right)
Vase with crackled green glaze derived from copper, CHINESE, about 1685-1725, (C.480-1910).
Small red buff earthenware bottle with Rouge Flambe glaze, ENGLISH, probably Burslem, Doulton's Factory, 1918, (C.379-1918).
Dull turquoise rectangular earthenware vase with unfired glaze, ENGLISH, Compton, Guildford, The Potter's Art Guild, about 1900-5, (C.144-1984).
Turquoise earthenware vase with dragon handles, ENGLISH, Maw and Company, 1871, (3403-1901).

PAGE 13
*Fan made of gold lacquer sticks with a painted mount, CHINESE, mid 19th century, (1622-1868).

PAGE 18
TOP: (Front)
Blue and white striped wine glass, ITALIAN, Venetian, late 16th or 17th century, (1822-1855).
(Back)
Two striped glass beer stines, GERMAN or NETHERLANDISH, 16th or 17th century, (587-1903 and 588-1903).
BOTTOM:
Two stoneware pots, ENGLISH, designed and made by Elizabeth Fritsch, small pot 1978, large pot 1980 (C.160a-1979 and C.13-1981).

PAGE 19
TOP: (Left to right)
Clear glass vase composed of parallel canes enclosing twisted pink and latticinio threads, ITALIAN, Venetian, 19th century, (4447-1901).
Glass beaker decorated with opaque red, white and blue threads, probably DUTCH, Amsterdam, Keizergracht factory, early 17th century, (1864-1855).
Glass jar made of welded glass canes containing white and multi-coloured filigree, ITALIAN, Venetian, late 16th or early 17th century, (1913A-1855).
MIDDLE:
Two fragments of striped glass, ROMAN, between 1st century BC and 1st century AD, (1077-68).
Three small bottles, probably Roman or Egyptian, 1st century B.C.
BOTTOM: (Right to left)
Tumbler made of welded glass canes containing white and yellow filigree alternating with pink stripes, ITALIAN, Venetian, late 16th or 17th century, (1822A-1855).
Mauve, blue and white striped glass vase, ITALIAN, Venetian, 17th century, (1862-1855).
Red and white glass bowl, ITALIAN,

Venetian, 17th or 18th century, (1819-1855).
Turquoise and white striped glass jug with metal top, ITALIAN, Venetian, 17th century, (C.203-1936).
Orange and white striped vase, CHINESE with enamelled decoration added in EUROPE, 18th century, (C.343A-1931).

PAGE 20
(Back)
Large blue, white and gold tin-glazed earthenware plate with twirling stripes, SPANISH, Catalonia, (360-1893).
(Middle row left to right)
Blue and white bowl with underglaze painting, PERSIAN, Kashan, about 1200-1221, (C.38-1947).
Little blue and white bowl with underglaze painting, PERSIAN, Kashan, about 1200-1221, (C.13-1913).
(Front)
White earthenware tankard with handle with decoration cut through black slip under a turquoise glaze, PERSIAN, 12th century, (C.725-1909).

PAGE 21
(Front row)
Fragments of striped glass (same as page 19).
Turquoise and black pot with underglaze decoration of fleur-de-lys, PERSIAN, about 1170-1220.
(Middle row left to right)
Small blue and white striped bowl with underglaze painting, PERSIAN, first half of 14th century, (C.703-1909).
Small camel and blue striped jug with underglaze painting, PERSIAN, Kashan, about 1200-1224, (C.752-1909).
(Back row left to right)
Green, sea-green, and yellow vase painted in opaque glazes, EGYPTIAN, Fatimid, 10th-12th centuries.
Large white earthenware bowl painted in blue, PERSIAN, Kashan, early 13th century, (C.49-1978).

PAGE 27
TOP: (Left to right)
Small glass tulip goblet, ENGLISH, 19th century.
Tall glass tulip goblet, ENGLISH, 19th century.

PAGES 40-41
Unfinished 'Tumbling Blocks' patchwork quilt, ENGLISH, 1860-70, (T.427-1980).
Tassels, star facetted pin cushion, star doily, pin cushion with red velvet top, embroidered hat and sewing box with pin cushion top all from V&A textile collection.

PAGE 44
BOTTOM LEFT:
'Mezzetin' and 'Lalage' characters from Italian comedy in porcelain enamelled and gilt, GERMAN, Nymphenburg, first modelled by Franz Anton Bustelli in 1760.
Snuffbox with diamond and flower designs in painted enamel on copper, ENGLISH. Staffordshire, 18th century.
Smaller figure in harlequin outfit in porcelain painted in enamel colours, ENGLISH, Bow, about 1760, (Schr.I.48).
Lead-glazed earthenware plate with enamel star decoration, ENGLISH, Staffordshire Burslem, Newport Pottery, design by Clarice Cliff, 1929-30, (C.75-1976).

PAGE 46
*Painting depicting Mahratta chief, Tulsaji of Tanjore (1765-88), riding horseback, SOUTH INDIAN, Mahratta school of Tanjore, about 1770, (IM.319-1921).

PAGE 52
TOP RIGHT AND LEFT:
*Part of panel of 31 tiles, made of earthenware and glazed and painted with a hexagonal geometric design, SYRIAN, Damascus, 15th century, (407-1898).
BOTTOM:
*Eight-pointed star and cross-shaped tiles from a panel of 15 earthenware tiles, PERSIAN, between 13th and 15th centuries, (1893-1897/546-1900).

PAGE 53
LEFT:
*Squares and triangles patchwork cover in satins, brocades and velvets, embroidered with silver thread and silk in satin, slim, long and short and chain stitches with couching and applied work, some of the squares with applied pictures illustrating scenes from Aesop's Fables, 6ft 3in by 4ft 5½in, ENGLISH, 18th century, (1475-1902).
TOP RIGHT:
*Porcelain harlequin family, GERMAN, Meissen, about 1740, (C.20-1984).
BOTTOM RIGHT:
*Porcelain harlequin with black and white face mask holding jug and hat, GERMAN, Meissen, about 1738, (C.106-1945).

PAGES 54-55
(Back row left to right)
Sea green jug with coloured glaze and ostrich motif moulded in relief, PERSIAN, 17th century, (641-1889).
Large cornflower blue ewer with coloured glaze and decoration moulded in relief, PERSIAN, 17th

century, (2643-1876).

Turquoise bottle with coloured glaze and turquoise flower motif moulded in relief, PERSIAN, 17th century, (711-1896).

Turquoise earthenware bottle with moulded decoration, coloured glazes and cream flower motif on burgundy background, PERSIAN, 17th century, (634-1889).

Large jade-green jug with leaf design and monochrome glaze, PERSIAN, 16th or 17th century, (2492A-1876).

(Front row left to right)
Gourd-shaped jug with opaque turquoise glaze, PERSIAN, probably 17th century, (621-1889).

Bowl with opaque royal blue glaze, PERSIAN, 17th century, (1014-1883).

Round blue bottle with openwork motif, moulded decoration and coloured glazes, PERSIAN, 17th century, (1298-1876).

Blue earthenware bottle with yellow flower motif and coloured glazes, PERSIAN, 17th century, (61-1302).

White earthenware bottle with turquoise tin glaze, PERSIAN, Kashan, early 13th century, (C.154-1977).

Small jade-green flask with monochrome glaze and leaf design in relief, PERSIAN, 16th or 17th century, (1348-1876).

Royal blue hookah-base with opaque glaze and silver spout, neck and top, PERSIAN, 17th century, (1296-1876).

PAGE 62
Glass fragments, probably Roman, 1st or 2nd century AD.

PAGES 64-65
Glass beads, ROMAN, probably 1st or 2nd century AD.

Glass fragments (same as page 62).

Two knives and two forks, ITALIAN, Venetian, 18th century, (1567-55, 1567A-55 and 2322-55).

PAGE 68
TOP:
Stoneware miniature vases, ENGLISH, Martin Brothers, 1901-1907, (left to right 487-1919, 427-1919, 483-1919, 425-1919 and 479-1919).

PAGE 70
TOP:
Glass paperweight of millefiori type, FRENCH, Baccarat, 1846, (427-1901).

PAGE 71
MIDDLE LEFT: (Left to right)
Snuff bottle in coralline limestone with brown ground, yellow spots and turquoise stopper, CHINESE, 18th or 19th century, (C.1806-1910).

Snuff bottle in coralline limestone with brown ground, white dots and

yellow stopper, CHINESE, 18th or 19th century, (C.1728-1910).

Snuff bottle in turquoise matrix with dark brown ground, turquoise spots and turquoise stopper, CHINESE, 18th or 19th century, (C.1595-1910).

PAGES 72-73
Four figures in 'egg-shell' porcelain painted over the glaze in enamel colours of the 'famille rose' holding lotus flower candlesticks, CHINESE, about 1730-50, (FE.23&A-1978, C.1194-1917 and C.1195-1917).

(Foreground)
Cup in form of a magnolia flower painted in enamel colours, CHINESE, 1907, (FE.12-1972).

(Back left to right)
Winepot painted over the glaze in enamel colours of the 'famille rose', CHINESE, 18th century, (C.1482&A-1910).

Pink porcelain vase painted over the glaze in enamel colours of the 'famille rose', CHINESE, reign of Qianlong, 1736-1795, (C.1399-1910).

PAGE 80
TOP LEFT:
Royal blue glass vase with large spots, ENGLISH, designed and made by Simon Moore, 1985, (C.209-1985).

PAGE 90
TOP LEFT:
*War painting illustrating the wounding of Khan Kilan by a Rayput, INDIAN, 1590, (IM.2-1896 88/117).

TOP RIGHT:
*Glass bowl with striped patches probably formed by interlaced canes of coloured glass, ROMAN, (969-1868).

BOTTOM:
*Squares carpet, 7ft 2in by 4ft 10in, PERSIAN, Bakhtiari, 19th century, (T.127-1928).

PAGE 91
TOP LEFT:
*Gameboard with ornate figures on chequerboard design made of papier mâché and signed 'for Edward VII', ENGLISH, about 1850, (W.26-1959).

TOP RIGHT:
*Patchwork quilt made of silk strips, ENGLISH, fabrics date from 1780's onwards, (T.117-1973).

BOTTOM LEFT:
*Table top made of mahogany and ebony with marble inlay, ENGLISH, designed by W. Chambers, 1769, (W.38-1977).

BOTTOM RIGHT:
*Circle and square patchwork made of printed cottons, ENGLISH, 1829 and later border, (T.428-1985).

PAGE 96

*Sion Gospels bookcover, beechwood overlaid with gold enriched with precious stones and cloisonné enamel, height 10in (25.4cm), GERMAN, about 11th century with additions of 12th century, (567-1893).

PAGES 100-101
(Left to right)
Gilt vase decorated with flowers, ENGLISH, Spode, 19th century, (C.703A-1935).

Tulip cup and saucer, ENGLISH, Spode, Staffordshire, about 1820, (C.720-1935).

Three-dimensional porcelain fruit and flowers, ENGLISH, Coalport, about 1830, (C.566-1935).

Punchbowl in soft-paste porcelain decorated with rust roses, ENGLISH, Derby, about 1820, (C.225-1938).

PAGE 102
TOP LEFT:
Detail of three-dimensional porcelain fruit and flowers, (same as pages 100-101).

TOP RIGHT:
Plate decorated with flowers and blue border, WELSH, Nantgarw, 1811-19, (C.76-1923).

BOTTOM LEFT:
Gilt vase decorated with flowers, ENGLISH, Spode, 19th century, (C.703-1935).

BOTTOM RIGHT:
Detail of plate decorated with basket of flowers, WELSH, Nantgarw, 1811-19, (3519-1901).

PAGE 103
BOTTOM:
Six cylindrical vases, ENGLISH, Swinton, Rockingham factory, about 1830, (C.765-1935, C.764-1935).

PAGE 106
TOP:
*Marquetry room panelling with flower and bird decoration, ENGLISH, 1686-88, (W.132-1919).

PAGE 114
TOP LEFT:
*Mirror back made of papier mâché with lacquered flower design, PERSIAN, made for the Paris exhibition, 1869, (922-1869).

BOTTOM:
*Stamped leather with flowers and small virgin and child in centre, ITALIAN, about 1700, (5901-1859).

PAGE 115
TOP:
*Painted wooden chimney board decorated with flowers in a blue and white pot, ENGLISH, about 1700, (W.35-1928).

PAGE 123
Cabbage bowl with cover, ENGLISH, Coalport, 19th century.

Cauliflower set of two teapots, tea caddy, creamer and plate, ENGLISH, Staffordshire, about 1760-5, (2272-1901, II.292, II.293, C.1242-1919, C.23-1940).

PAGE 124
Plate decorated with fruit, ENGLISH, Derby, painted by T. Steele, 1810-30, (3036-1901).

PAGE 125
LEFT-HAND COLUMN: (Top to bottom)
Porcelain plate with three-dimensional peas, ENGLISH, Minton, about 1820, (414-1885/810A).

Asparagus dish with lid, GERMAN, Meissen, late 18th century.

Melon tureen and cover, ENGLISH, Chelsea, about 1755, (2938&A-1901).

Plate decorated with melons and flowers, (same as page 3).

PAGES 128-129
(Back row left to right)
Large yellow porcelain vase painted in enamel colours with moulded decoration, ENGLISH, Bristol, about 1770, (C.614-1935).

White porcelain 'frill' vase for pot pourri painted with enamel colours, ENGLISH, Derby, late 18th century.

Large yellow vase with openwork neck, ENGLISH, Bristol, about 1770, (C.613-1935).

Porcelain cane handle painted in enamels and gilt, ENGLISH, Lowestoft, about 1780, (C.663-1925).

Lady with turban pipe, CONTINENTAL, 18th century, (C.819-1956).

Ceramic flower dessert basket painted in enamel colours and gilt, ENGLISH, London, Worcester, about 1770, decorated in workshops of James Giles, (Schr.I.545).

Little blue teacup decorated with three-dimensional leaves and flowers, ENGLISH, Coalport, about 1830, (C.428-1915).

PAGE 134
(From top to bottom left to right)
African man with turban snuffbox, ENGLISH, 18th century.

Lady with turban pipe, (same as pages 128-9).

Sun head detail from earthenware puzzle-jug, ENGLISH, Staffordshire, early 19th century, (2633-1901).

Detail of face with flowers from white vase (same as pages 128-9).

Detail of angel heads on earthenware drug-vase, ITALIAN, 1525, (523-1865).

Detail from large yellow porcelain vase, (same as pages 128-9, C.614-

1935).

Woman with pink cheeks snuffbox, ENGLISH, 18th century.

Dog's head porcelain snuffbox with gilt mounts, DANISH, about 1795, (343-1902).

Angry man's head with beard snuff-box, ENGLISH, 18th century.

PAGE 135

TOP: (Left to right)
Laughing head porcelain pipe bowl, GERMAN, Nymphenburg, about 1757, (C.57-1956).

*Portrait of Queen Elizabeth, case in enamelled gold set with rubies and diamonds, ENGLISH, by Nicholas Hilliard, 16th century, (4404-1857).

MIDDLE: (Left to right)
*Self portrait, ENGLISH, by Nicholas Hilliard, 16th century, (P.154-1910).

Ceramic woman's head with bonnet, ENGLISH, Chelsea, 1749-54, (Schreiber collection I.231).

*Portrait of Richard Hilliard, ENGLISH, by Nicholas Hilliard, 1577, (P.154-1910).

BOTTOM: (Left to right)
*Masker's apron made of embroidered silks, TIBETAN, 19th century, (IS.499B-1905).

Man's head with beard wine jug, ENGLISH, Burslem, by Ralph Wood II, about 1790, (Schreiber collection II.309).

Ceramic bonbonnière of head with fur hat, ENGLISH, Chelsea, about 1765, (Schreiber collection I.274).

PAGE 138

TOP: (Left to right)
*Painted green bird with pink flowers and butterfly, INDIAN, Mughal, about 1625, (IS.218-1951).

*Painting of lapwing, INDIAN, Mughal, Delhi, about 1800 but copy of 17th century original, (IM.126A-1921).

*Wallpaper decorated in pen, watercolour and gouache, CHINESE, early 19th century, (E.3592-1922 and E.409-1932).

MIDDLE LEFT:
*Painting of 2 doves, INDIAN, Kalighat, about 1830, (IS.213-1950).

BOTTOM:
*Embroidered sampler, MEXICAN, late 18th or early 19th century, (T.91-1954).

PAGE 139

TOP:
*Shell patchwork quilt, ENGLISH, late 18th century, (242-1908).

MIDDLE LEFT:
*Enamelled dish with fish decoration, FRENCH, about 1905, (Metalwork).

MIDDLE RIGHT:
Fish tureen, cover and stand in enamelled colours, ENGLISH, Chelsea,

about 1756, (C.1451 to b-1924).

BOTTOM RIGHT:
Detail of painted fish from vase decorated in red enamel and gilt with powdered blue ground, CHINESE, reign of K'ang Hsi, 1662-1722, (199-1905).

PAGES 140-141

(Back row left to right)
Tin-glazed earthenware with blue tree, ENGLISH, Wincanton, Somerset, late 18th century, (Circ.415-1950).

Tin-glazed earthenware plate with blue figure and mountain, ENGLISH, mid 18th century, (Circ.905-1924).

(Middle row left to right)
Tin-glazed earthenware blue and white plate with dark blue border, ENGLISH, Lambeth, about 1750, (C.72-1965).

Blue and white plate with Chinese figure sitting under tree, ENGLISH, Liverpool, about 1750, (C.79-1965).

(Front row left to right)
Tin-glazed earthenware plate decorated with stencilled flowers and scratched designs, ENGLISH, 18th century, (C.73-1957).

Tin-glazed earthenware dish decorated with fish, ENGLISH, Bristol or Liverpool, about 1760, (C.75-1965).

(Foreground left to right)
Two tin-glazed earthenware tiles painted blue and mauve, ENGLISH Delftware, 18th century, (C.116H-1981, C.126D-1981).

Tin-glazed earthenware tile painted blue, DUTCH Delftware, 17th or 18th century, (C.577-1923/108C5).

PAGE 145

(Back left to right)
Blue and white drinking vessel painted in underglaze blue and black, PERSIAN, 17th century, (429-1878).

Blue and white bottle, PERSIAN, 18th century, (1245-76).

(Front left to right)
Blue and white jug with lid, DUTCH, Delft, about 1700, (C.268-1923).

Round blue and white hookah-base painted in underglaze blue and black, PERSIAN, 17th century, (988-1883).

Small blue and white jar with bird motifs around neck, PERSIAN, 16th or 17th century, (2452-1876).

Blue and white bottle with Chinese figures, PERSIAN, 18th century, (1845-1876).

PAGES 152-153

(Back left to right)
Blue and white porcelain vase painted in underglaze blue, CHINESE, 17th century, (769-1885).

Blue, white and yellow jug plate, DUTCH or GERMAN, 17th or 18th century, (C.60-1966).

Tall blue and white vase with lid and a garniture painted in underglaze blue, ENGLISH, Worcester, about 1765-70, (720B-1907).

(Front left to right)
Small blue and white cream jug with handle and river landscape painted in underglaze blue, CHINESE, about 1770, (FE.32-1977).

Small blue and white porcelain saucer painted in underglaze blue, CHINESE, reign of K'ang Hsi, 1662-1722, (C.43&A-1955).

Blue and white miniature porcelain jar and pot, CHINESE, reign of K'ang Hsi, 1662-1722, (C.16-1909, C.18-1909).

Blue and white porcelain stem cup painted in underglaze blue, CHINESE, Jiaping reign, 1522-66, (C.120-1928).

Vase decorated with small boys playing among scrolling lotus, CHINESE, about 1630-50, (C.107-1928).

YARN AND KIT INFORMATION

BUYING YARN

Most of the instructions for Kaffe Fassett knitting and needlepoint designs included in the preceding pages specify the type of yarn used. If possible, it is best to use the yarn specified (addresses for Rowan and Appleton yarns follow). When a specific yarn is not given in the knitting instructions or when the reader wishes to use a different brand of yarn, the suggested general yarn weight should be used as a guide for substitution. If in doubt about how to make a substitute yarn choice, obtain assistance from your local yarn shop for substituting yarns.

KAFFE FASSETT KITS

The following Kaffe Fassett needlepoint and knitting designs which appear in the book are available as kits. The knitting kits are widely available in yarn shops. For further information on stockists and for a list of the full range of Kaffe Fassett kits and knitting patterns contact Rowan Yarns. Needlepoint kits are available mail order from Ehrman (addresses follow).

NEEDLEPOINT KITS

KNITTING KITS

KAFFE FASSETT WALLPAPER

For information on Kaffe Fassett wallpaper contact Ehrman (addresses follow).

APPLETON YARNS

Appleton needlepoint yarns are widely available in needlework shops. For further information on stockists contact the following:

UK and EUROPE: Appleton Bros Ltd, Thames Works, Church Street, Chiswick, London W4 2PE. Tel: (01) 994 0711

USA: American Crewel and Canvas Studio, PO Box 453, 164 Canal Street, Canastota, NY 13032. Tel: (315) 697 3759

EHRMAN

UK and EUROPE: Ehrman, 21/22 Vicarage Gate, London W8 4AA, England. Tel: (01) 937 4568

AUSTRALIA: Sunspun Enterprises Pty Ltd, 195 Canterbury Road, Canterbury, Victoria 3126. Tel: (03) 830 1609

CANADA: Estelle Designs and Sales Ltd, 38 Continental Place, Scarborough, Ontario M1R 2T4. Tel: (416) 298 9922

DENMARK: Mosekonens Vaerksted, Mosevej 13, Li Binderup, 9600 Aars. Tel: 45 8 656065

FRANCE: Armada, Collange, Lourmand, 71250 Cluny. Tel: 85 59 1356

NEW ZEALAND: R.G. & P.A. Hoddinott, PO Box 1486, Auckland.

SWEDEN: T.I.D.A., Box 2055, S-103 12 Stockholm. Tel: 468 103355

USA: The Westminster Trading Corporation, 5 Northern Boulevard, Amherst, NH 03031. Tel: (603) 886 5174

ROWAN YARNS

Rowan yarns are widely available in yarn shops. For further information on stockists and mail order sources contact the following:

UK and EUROPE: Rowan Yarns, Green Lane Mill, Holmfirth, West Yorksire HD7 1RW, England. Tel: (0484) 686714/687374

AUSTRALIA: Sunspun Enterprises Pty Ltd, 195 Canterbury Road, Canterbury, Victoria 3126. Tel: (03) 830 1609

CANADA: Estelle Designs and Sales

INDEX

Knitting and needlepoint designs with full instructions are listed below in **bold**.

Ltd, 38 Continental Place, Scarborough, Ontario M1R 2T4. Tel: (416) 298 9922
BERMUDA: The Yarn Loft, P.O. Box DV 203, Devonshire DV BX. Tel: 809 29 5 0551
CYPRUS: Colourworks, 12 Parnithos Street, Nicosia. Tel: 357 472933
DENMARK: Mosekonens Vaerksted, Mosevej 13, Li Binderup, 9600 Aars. Tel: 45 8 656065
HOLLAND: Henk & Henrietta Beukers, Dorpsstraat 9, 5327 AR Hurwenen. Tel: 31 4182 1764
ITALY: La Compagnia Del Cotone, Sede Legale, Corso Matteotti, 35-10121 Torino. Tel: (011) 878381

JAPAN: DiaKeito Co. Ltd., 1-5-23 Nkatsu, Oyodo-Ku, Osaka 531. Tel: 06 371 5653
NEW ZEALAND: Creative Fashion Centre, P.O. Box 45083, Epuni Railway, Lower Hutt. Tel: (04) 664 689
NORWAY: Eureka, Kvakkestandgarden, 1400 Ski. Tel: 0287 1909
SWEDEN: Wincent, Luntmakargatan 56, 113 58 Stockholm.
WEST GERMANY: Textilwerkstatt, Friedenstrasse 5, 3000 Hanover 1. Tel: (0511) 818001
USA: The Westminster Trading Corporation, 5 Northern Boulevard, Amherst, NH 03031. Tel: (603) 886 5041

KNITTING ABBREVIATIONS

approx	*approximately*	patt(s)	*pattern(s)*
beg	*begin(ning)*	psso	*pass slip stitch over*
cm	*centimetre(s)*	rem	*remain(s)(ing)*
cont	*continu(e)(ing)*	rep	*repeat(s)(ing)*
dec	*decreas(e)(ing)*	RS	*right side(s)*
foll	*follow(s)(ing)*	sl	*slip*
g	*gramme(s)*	sl st	*slip stitch*
inc	*increas(e)(ing)*	st(s)	*stitch(es)*
"	*inch(es)*	st st	*stocking (stockinette) stitch*
K	*knit*	tbl	*through back of loop(s)*
m	*metre(s)*	tog	*together*
oz	*ounce(s)*	WS	*wrong side(s)*
P	*purl*	yd	*yard(s)*

ACKNOWLEDGEMENTS

After the sustained team effort of putting this book together, I feel quite a sham for allowing my name to head the cover. I take great pleasure therefore in naming some of the many contributions to this work.

First of all thank you to Sir Roy Strong for his encouragement over the years and for sanctioning the exhibition at the V&A which led to this book and to HRH Princess Michael of Kent for suggesting it. Thank you to Ehrman, Rowan Yarns and Century for backing the exhibition so generously.

To the Ceramic, Oriental and Textile Departments of the V&A for their hours of assistance a special thank you. To Garth Hall and his team thank you for help on planning and setting up the exhibition.

For hours of dedicated knitting and stitching thanks go to Rory Mitchell, Kay Kettles, Zoë Hunt, Maria Brannan, Diana Hutton, Caroline Day, Elian McCready, Barry McGinn, Bea Berry, June Henry and Julia Lewandowskyj.

For help with patterns and yarns thanks to Kathleen and Kim Hargreaves and Linda Clarke at Rowan Yarns.

Thank you to Kay Gallwey for some of the styling in the fashion shots and to all our models, especially to Richard, James and Zoë. Thank you to *Browns* for loan of clothes, to *Putnams* and *Heraz* for loan of props and fabrics and to Mrs. Quaddy at *Pulbrook and Gould* for helping with flowers.

A huge thank you to chief cook and business partner Richard Womersley, without whose support we would never have made the deadline.

Thanks to Sally Harding for editing so creatively and to Cherriwyn Magill for the complicated task of art editing this diverse lot!

Thanks also to Sarah Wallace for keeping us all at it and Gabrielle for the V&A research.

And finally a very grateful acknowledgement of the boundless creative input of Steve Lovi who orchestrated this book on every level.

WITHDRAWN

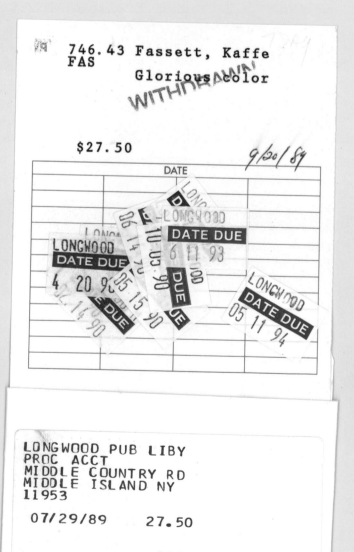